Chemo, Craziness & Comfort

My book about childhood cancer

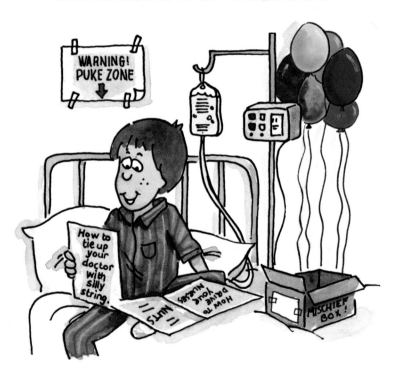

Words by Nancy Keene
Pictures by Trevor Romain

...because kids can't fight cancer alone!

Candlelighters
Childhood Cancer Foundation

Chemo, Craziness And Comfort: My book about childhood cancer
By Nancy Keene and Trevor Romain

Copyright © 2002 Candlelighters Childhood Cancer Foundation
Printed in the United States of America

Published by Candlelighters Childhood Cancer Foundation

Editor: Mary Ellen Keene

Copy Editors: Doris Keene & Ruth Hoffman

Production Editor: Ruth Hoffman

Cover Design: Trevor Romain and Dick Reeves

Orbie Copyright: 2002 Trevor Romain

Printing History: October 2002 First Edition

ISBN 0-9724043-0-9

...because kids can't fight cancer alone!

Candlelighters™
Childhood Cancer Foundation

Table of Contents

Introduction

Hi! This book is for kids with cancer. We know that kids are really baby goats and that children are humans. But kids call themselves kids, so we do too.

We thought we'd tell you a little bit about ourselves and why we wrote this book. Nancy wrote the words; Trevor drew the pictures. Nancy's daughter Kathryn had leukemia when she was 3. She's 14 now and in middle school. She was diagnosed on Valentine's Day, 1992, so she gets to have a double celebration on that day every year. Kathryn likes computer games, reading, and ice-skating. Nancy likes taking care of her kids (Kathryn and younger sister Alison), reading books, playing with her puppy, and telling bad jokes (this becomes obvious in the book).

Nancy has written several books for parents of children with cancer. But, she thought that kids needed their own book.

Trevor writes books for kids and does all of the illustrations. His books have titles like "Bullies are a Pain in the Brain" and "How to do Homework without Throwing Up." He's a very funny man. He likes kids with cancer and spends a lot of time at his local hospital doing fun stuff with them. They call him Dr. Mischief there. One time he had all the kids put their clothes on backwards and he painted faces on the back of their bald heads. Trevor also enjoys traveling around the world speaking at schools, conferences, hospitals and anywhere else people and pets will listen to him.

We (Trevor and Nancy) both know that cancer is serious. But we also believe that you can find ways to deal with it and still do your regular kid stuff like play with your friends, go to school, and ride your bike around the neighborhood. One way to figure out how to cope with something hard is to learn all about it. If you understand what cancer is and what the treatments are, it helps. If you get tips on things to make it easier, it helps a lot.

That's what this book is for. We want to help you (and your parents and brothers and sisters) understand about cancer, how it's treated, and ways to manage it. Thousands of children in the United States (over 12,000!) are diagnosed with cancer each year. So, you have lots of company. This book shares stories and advice from kids who have finished their treatments. They wanted to help you get through the treatments so that you can make each day the best it can be.

Each chapter has a page at the end where you can draw pictures or write down questions for your doctor. One way to understand something is to ask lots of questions. And since this is your book, you can write all over it if you want. You can just read the parts you want to. Some kids like to read every word and others only read the parts that interest them. Others might want to draw pictures and ignore the words. It's up to you.

Some kids like to have their parents read it to them. Others like to crawl under their blankets in bed and read it by themselves with a flashlight. Since this is your book, you can do whatever you want. But if you have any questions, ask a doctor or nurse or child life specialist (they are the ones with the toys and games). If you feel shy or embarrassed or too sick to ask questions, you can get your mom or dad to ask them for you. Just make sure they tell you the answers.

At the back of the book is a packing list of things to bring to the hospital. It might give you some ideas of things to pack that will help pass the time. There is also a journal for you to write in whenever you want. It's a way to remember your hospital roommates and also to write about your feelings. You can draw pictures instead of writing if you would prefer that. After all, this is your book.

We are very, very sorry that you got cancer. It is a hard thing. But, we hope this little book will make it easier for you.

Hugs from

Trevor and Nancy and Orbie.

Thank You

This book wouldn't exist if Ruth Hoffman, Executive Director of Candlelighters Childhood Cancer Foundation, hadn't thought of the idea, talked Nancy and Trevor into doing it, and then raised the money to make it happen. She then encouraged everyone involved and helped shepherd the writing, editing, and illustrating through all of the inevitable rough spots. She oversaw the many details about printing, covers, and shipping. She is both highly competent and a delight to work with. She's the best!

A generous contribution from the Davenport Family Foundation made this book possible. We give our deepest thanks for their support that enabled us to create a helpful book for the littlest of cancer warriors.

Huge thanks to the following groups that made generous donations to this project:
Candlelighters of Brevard, Inc.; Melbourne, Florida
Candlelighters for Children with Cancer; Oregon & SW
    Washington
Inland NW Candlelighters; Spokane, WA
Candlelighters Childhood Cancer Foundation of
    Western Washington
CURE Childhood Cancer; Atlanta, GA
Candlelighters of the El Paso Area; El Paso, TX
Childhood Cancer Lifeline of New Hampshire
Candlelighters of Cook Children's; Fort Worth, TX
Candlelighters Childhood Cancer Network; Pittsburgh, PA
Candlelighters Family Support Group; Chattanooga, TN
Families of Children with Cancer, Inc.; Oneida, WI
Hawaii Children's Cancer Foundation; Honolulu, HI
Candlelighters of the University of Missouri; Columbia, MO

Thank you to Dick Reeves for the gorgeous design and layout of the book. We couldn't have done it without you. A big thanks to Mary Ellen Keene and Doris Keene for editing and copyediting the book. Their personal knowledge and editorial skills made the book much better. They are both always ports in a storm.

Lots of kids, parents, doctors, nurses, and psychologists read this book. They caught mistakes, made suggestions, and pointed out things we forgot to include.

We would like to extend a hug and a big thank you to:

The kids

Elizabeth Glaze
Sarah Hammer
Jon Hammer
Abe Kline
Ethan Kline

Jake Kline
Tucker Kline
Alison Leake
Kathryn Leake
Jamie Vizena

The grownups

Ricky Carroll
Roxie Glaze
Ruth Hoffman
Wendy Hobbie CRNP
Kathleen Ingman PhD
F. Leonard Johnson MD
Marcio Malogolowkin MD
Grace Monaco JD

Pat Reynolds MD PhD
Mary Rourke PhD
Kathy Ruccione RN MPH
Tania Shiminski-Maher CPNP
Anne Spurgeon
Elaine Vizena
Catherine Woodman MD
Joe Zins PhD

We so appreciate everyone's help for this much-needed book. It was truly a community effort.

"We can do no great things – only small things with great love."

Mother Teresa

CHAPTER 1

Your Healthy Body

Y ou are special. Although there are billions of people in the world, not a single one is just like you. Some people are tall, and some are short. Some have blue eyes, and some have brown. Some have big belly laughs and others smile shyly when they see or hear something funny. And some kids get cancer and others don't.

This book is for you and other kids who have cancer. Your mom and dad, brothers and sisters, friends and teachers might also want to read it to help them understand about cancer and its treatment. Cancer is when one little part of your body starts acting in a way it shouldn't. To help understand what's going on, let's first talk about healthy bodies.

Your body

When you look in the mirror, what do you see? Hair and a face and skin? Someone with a nice smile and a pug nose? Do you see a person who likes to play in the ocean or paint pictures?

Hi, I'm Orbie.
I'm here to help you understand a crazy disease called cancer and to help make your journey through treatment a lot easier.

Do you ever wonder about the parts of your body that are under your skin? This chapter talks about different parts of your body. But how you feel about your body and what's happening to it are also part of who you are. As you read, be sure to ask your mother, father, grandparents, doctor, or nurse if you have any questions.

Cells

A cell is a small bit of you that is unique. Before you were born, you were just one cell inside your mother. That one cell was smaller than the period at the end of this sentence, but in it was a map for making you. The one cell grew a bit then divided into two cells. These two cells divided again and again until now you are made up of millions and millions of cells. The great grandchildren of your original cell are now brain cells, muscle cells, fingernail cells and all of the other cells in your body.

Even though there are many different types of cells in your body, they each have the same set of instructions, called genes. If you looked through a very powerful microscope, your genes would look like beads on a string. Each bead is a gene, and when they are strung together they are called DNA. Long strings of DNA are in every cell in your body. When a new cell is made, your body copies the DNA so that each new cell has the same instructions. You are special because no other person (or animal or plant!) has the exact same set of genes that you do (unless you have an identical twin).

Bones and joints

Take a moment and squeeze your arm. Under your skin are muscles, and inside the muscles are bones. 206 hard bones (your skeleton) form a frame inside your body to keep you from collapsing into a soggy heap. Your skeleton also helps keep the various organs in your body in the places they belong. For instance, you can't lose your brain since the skull (made of bone) keeps it where is should be.

Some bones are long and strong (thigh bone) while others are tiny (bone in the tip of your little finger). Others are flat and wide (shoulder blade). Bones are not solid, like a chocolate bar. Most have a space inside that contains bone marrow— a sticky material that makes blood cells. At the end of most bones, the inside looks like honeycomb. This is the area (called epiphysis) that grows as you get older. Bones also store minerals like calcium that are released whenever your body needs them.

You can swing a baseball bat, bend your knees, and nod your head because your bones are linked together by movable joints. If two hard bones constantly rubbed together, they would soon wear out. But our bodies are designed to last a lifetime. A smooth, long-lasting substance called cartilage covers the bone ends at joints. Just as the chain on your bike needs oil to work smoothly, so do joints. The "oil" your body uses in joints is called synovial fluid.

Muscles

Stretch your arms high over your head. Can you feel your muscles moving in your arms and shoulders? You have over 600 muscles in your body, that control movements from kicking a ball to making your heart beat. Some muscles you know about, like the ones in your legs that help you run and jump. Others, like those in your chest, help you breathe without your even thinking about it.

There are three main types of muscles: skeletal, smooth, and cardiac. Muscles attached to the bones are called skeletal muscles. The muscles in your legs are skeletal muscles. The layers of muscles in internal organs, like the stomach, are smooth. They contract to push food through your stomach and intestines. The walls of the heart are made of cardiac muscle. This muscle squeezes about once every second to pump blood throughout your body.

Lungs

Take a deep breath. Do you know what happens every time you breathe? Fresh air enters your body through your nose or mouth. It goes down a tube called a windpipe into your lungs. Your lungs are two big organs in your chest that look like wet, pink sponges. Inside are thousands of tiny air sacs with very thin walls. The oxygen in the air you breathe goes through the walls of the air sacs into the blood in tiny veins. Your blood carries the oxygen to every cell in your body. Your cells need oxygen to stay alive and healthy.

If your body needs more oxygen, you breathe faster and take deeper breaths without even having to think about it. When you play soccer or run around in gym class, you probably start breathing faster and faster. This helps your cells get enough oxygen to do the extra work you need them to do.

Blood and blood vessels

Your body has an amazing network of vessels that carries blood to every single cell. Some of these vessels are like hoses the size of a pencil, but others are so tiny they are only as wide as the lead in a pencil. When your heart beats, it pushes blood around your body. If you press your pointer finger down on the inside of your wrist, you can feel a pulse of blood moving though a blood vessel. This pulse happens every time your heart squeezes.

Blood looks red because it is full of millions of red blood cells. Red blood cells carry oxygen to all of the other cells in your body, and they also carry carbon dioxide back to the lungs to be breathed out of your body.

Your blood contains a lot of other cells too. Tiny, dish-shaped cells, called platelets, clump together to stop bleeding if you cut your skin. More and more platelets stick together until you have a scab to protect your skin while your body repairs the damage. The blood is full of white blood cells, too. These are the body's army of defense. They catch and destroy any invaders like bacteria or viruses that could make you sick.

Blood also picks up food from your intestines and brings it to all of your body's cells. The cells then use oxygen and food to make energy. This energy helps you run, jump, and play.

Lymph

Did you know that your body has another network of vessels that carry a colorless liquid called lymph? It's true. The lymphatic system absorbs liquid that seeps out of cells and blood and returns it to the blood. It also carries infection-fighting white cells that gobble up bacteria and viruses to help you stay healthy.

Scattered throughout the lymph system are bean-shaped lymph nodes. These are full of white cells that snag any foreign invaders, like bacteria or viruses, that flow by. Have you ever had a lump on your

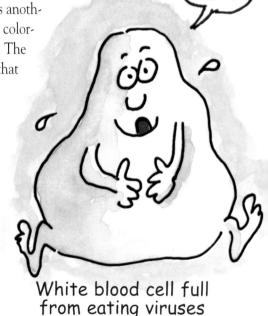

White blood cell full from eating viruses and bacteria.

neck that felt sore? Your doctor might have said you have "swollen lymph nodes." When you are sick, your body makes extra white cells that work very hard to destroy the foreign invaders. When many white cells get plump from eating lots of viruses and bacteria, your nodes can swell uncomfortably.

Your spleen is the biggest organ in your immune system. It's a little above your belly button but on the left side. The spleen gets rid of old red cells and platelets so that the new cells can do their jobs. It also stores some cells and helps your body fight off invaders.

Digestive system

Bodies need food to grow and thrive, so you have to eat. Do you ever wonder what happens to all of the sandwiches, fruits, and desserts you gobble up? Well, when you bite off a piece of food and chew it up, it gets mixed with a liquid called saliva (spit). Saliva comes from glands that are under the skin behind and below your mouth. It makes the food soft and moist.

When you swallow, the food goes down a long tube (the

esophagus) into your stomach. Your stomach is like a bag made of muscle. Acids and other substances in the stomach break the food down into smaller parts. The muscles in the stomach mix the food up (like a blender) until it turns into a liquid. It is then squeezed into a long tube called the small intestine. Juices in the small intestine break the small bits of liquid food into tiny particles that pass through the walls of the intestine into the blood. By the time the liquid reaches the end of the small intestine, most of the usable food has gone through the intestinal walls into your blood. What is left moves into the 5-foot long large intestine. Here water, vitamins, and minerals are absorbed. What is left over is solid waste (poop) that leaves the body through the anus.

Kidneys

Your body also needs to get rid of fluids it doesn't need. Two organs called kidneys do this. You have one kidney on the right side of your body and one on the left, a little bit below your ribcage. They are shaped like kidney beans and are about the size of your fist. The kidneys filter out waste products from the blood. This liquid waste, called urine, then flows into the bladder, where it remains until you go to the bathroom to urinate (pee).

When you gotta go, you gotta go!

Glands

Have you ever noticed how your heart thumps and you breathe fast when you watch a scary movie? This happens when your endocrine system is doing its job. Organs all over your body called glands release chemicals (called hormones) into your blood to keep all the systems in your body running smoothly.

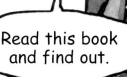

Scary movies can make a person's heart race.

Why?

Read this book and find out.

You have several endocrine glands and they each make different hormones. The adrenal glands, which sit on top of your kidneys, prepare your body to spring into action in emergencies. The thyroid is a butterfly-shaped gland in your neck. It helps you grow and also helps store the right amount of calcium in your bones. The male glands (testes) start to release hormones when boys become teenagers. These hormones help boys grow into men with deep voices and hair on their faces (beards). Female glands are the ovaries, located in the belly. Ovaries release hormones that help girls develop into women. The hypothalamus and pituitary are tiny glands deep in your brain that work together to control all of the other glands in your body.

Brain and nerves

After reading about all of the incredible parts of your body, you might wonder how it works so well. How can it always know to pull your finger away if it touches a hot stove or how does it remember to make your heart beat every second? The part of your body that keeps all of your complicated systems working smoothly is your brain.

Your brain is like a powerful computer that controls everything your body does. It takes in data from your eyes, ears, skin, and muscles and decides what to do. It controls how you think and what you remember. Your brain looks like a wrinkled walnut with two halves. Because the nerves in your brain cross over, the left side of your brain controls the right side of your body.

Different parts of your brain have different jobs. Your cerebral cortex is the thinking part and the cerebellum helps you keep your balance. The brain stem oversees automatic actions like breathing and heartbeat.

Your brain talks to the rest of your body through nerves. You have about fifty miles of nerves throughout your body. They relay information between your brain and the rest of your body using electrical signals. Your brain and nerves coordinate all of the other systems in your body. Isn't your body amazing?

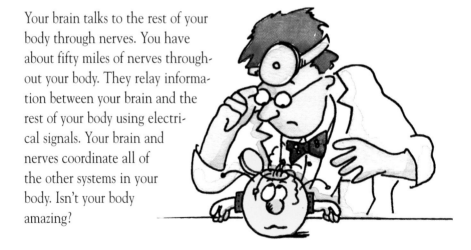

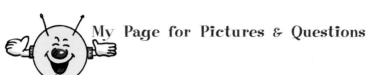 My Page for Pictures & Questions

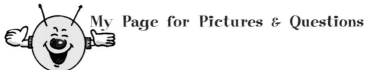 My Page for Pictures & Questions

Chapter 2

Your Body and Cancer

All kinds of people get cancer—from newborn babies to 90-year-old great grandparents. Wild animals and fish and pets also can get cancer. You might have a friend or know someone in your neighborhood who had cancer. But now your parents and doctor say you have it. And you're probably wondering, what is it, anyway?

When your body is healthy, cells all over your body follow the rules. They stay where they are supposed to and do their jobs. Your white blood cells protect you from infection. Your brain cells live in your brain and help you think.

Move out dude, we're moving in!

HEALTHY CELL

Your muscle cells stay put in the muscles and help you move.

When a cell, anywhere in your body, stops doing what it is supposed to do and starts making copies of itself, that's cancer. These cells divide over and over until there are way too many of them. They make lumps called tumors or fill up the insides of bones so that healthy cells get crowded out. Your healthy cells have a hard time doing their jobs. The cancer cells can start to spread around your body, cause all sorts of trouble, and make you sick.

Who gets it?

About 12,400 young people from birth to 19 years old get cancer every year in the United States. You may even have friends or classmates who had cancer. Children and teens get all different kinds of cancers, although the most common are leukemias and brain tumors. Different kinds of cancers are more common at certain ages. For instance, almost all children diagnosed with retinoblastoma, a cancer of the eye, are younger than 5. Most of the people diagnosed with osteosarcoma, a cancer of the bone, are teenagers.

What causes it?

Cancer is not just one disease. There are many different kinds, and many variations of each kind. It makes sense then, that there is not just one cause of cancer. Very little is known about the causes of cancers that strike children.

Some kids who get cancer think that something they said or did caused it. They say or think things like:

- If I drank all my milk like my mom told me to, I wouldn't have cancer.
- This cancer is a punishment for not doing my homework.
- If I had been nicer to the new baby, I'd still be healthy.

Very little is known about why some kids get cancer and other's don't.

The truth is, nothing you did (or didn't do) caused your cancer. Even saying the meanest things in the world doesn't cause cancer. Scientists and doctors still don't understand exactly what causes most kinds of kids' cancers, but they do know it isn't children's behavior. Just like you can't control whether your heart beats or not, you can't control whether you get cancer or not. It's a fact. Let's put that in big letters because its very important: IT'S NOT YOUR FAULT!

It's not your fault!

Sometimes brothers and sisters feel guilty if they got mad and said, "I hope you get sick." Sometimes they'll say they wish you were never born, and the next thing they know, you are in the hospital. They are not so powerful that their words caused your cancer. Nobody's words can cause cancer. Thoughts, either. Or even wishes. Let's put that in big letters too: YOUR BROTHER OR SISTER DIDN'T CAUSE YOUR CANCER!

Parents often feel guilty too. They sometimes think if they hadn't used chemicals on their lawn that their child wouldn't have cancer. The truth is, though, that not much is known about what causes childhood cancer. There is nothing they could have done to prevent it. YOUR PARENTS CANNOT PREVENT CANCER!

Why you have cancer is a mystery, and sometimes mysteries are hard to accept. But the truth is, you didn't cause your cancer, your brother or sister didn't cause it, and neither did your parents. Maybe in the future, scientists will know enough about causes so that they can prevent children from ever getting cancer. But in the meantime, what's most important is to work with your family and doctors and nurses to get treatments so you can start to get better.

The rest of this chapter describes the types of cancer that children get. They are listed in alphabetical order to make it easier for you to find your type of cancer. These short descriptions tell a little bit about each cancer, how many kids in the U.S. are diagnosed every year, and how each cancer is treated. This is an introduction to your cancer. Your doctors and nurses can give you lots more information and answer any questions you have.

In the beginning, children and parents think of lots of questions and then sometimes forget what they wanted to ask. When people are tired and shocked, their brains don't hold on to information as well as usual. This is normal. Some parents and kids write down their questions so that they have a list ready when they see the doctor. After reading about your cancer, you can write down your questions on the page at the end of the chapter.

Brain and spinal cord tumors

Tumors can grow in any part of the brain or the spinal cord. There are many, many different kinds of tumors that can grow in the brain. Some grow slowly and some grow very fast. Some are in parts of the brain that are hard to reach and others are routinely removed during operations. All tumors in the brain can affect the way you think or move.

In the U.S., about 2,200 children younger than 19 are diagnosed each year with brain or spinal cord tumors. Since there are so many different kinds of tumors, the number of children with each kind is very small.

Treatment is improving for children with brain and spinal cord tumors. Doctors now use sophisticated computers to help them during surgery and when giving radiation. Powerful microscopes help them see the brain when they operate.

Most children and teens with brain or spinal cord tumors need surgery. The surgeon may take a small piece of the tumor (biopsy) to view under the microscope. Surgeons also sometimes take out part of the tumor or the entire tumor during an operation. Occasionally, surgery is used to put radiation implants in the tumor. In other cases, the tumor is in a place that surgeons can't reach without hurting important parts of the brain. So, they don't remove it. Instead, they use radiation or chemotherapy to get rid of it.

Radiation is used for many types of tumors in the brain or spinal cord. Sometimes the radiation is aimed only at the tumor. Other times, the whole brain needs radiation in case little bits of the tumor have traveled to other parts of the brain. The amount of radiation and how often you need it depends on the type of tumor, where it is located, and how old you are. Doctors try to avoid or postpone the use of radiation in children under 3 years old.

Chemotherapy (drugs that kill cancer cells) is also used to treat some types of brain tumors.

Ewing's sarcoma

Ewing's sarcomas can grow in bones or soft tissues. There are three different kinds of sarcomas with big names, but they are similar when looked at under a microscope. The three types of Ewing's sarcomas are Ewing's sarcoma, extraosseous Ewing's sarcoma (EES), and primitive neuroductal tumor (PNET). These tumors can grow in arms, legs, or the middle parts of your body, such as your hip bones.

About 200 children and teens in the U.S. are diagnosed with one of these tumors every year. Most of them (almost 90%) have a Ewing's sarcoma in the bone. Some children get Ewing's sarcoma at ages 5 to 10, but most develop this type of cancer after the age of 11.

In the last twenty years, treatment for Ewing's sarcoma has changed and improved. The only option used to be removing the part of the body with the tumor (called amputation). Now, doctors usually use chemotherapy followed by surgery or radiation.

All children or teens with Ewing's sarcoma need surgery. Sometimes amputation is necessary. But, there are really great substitute limbs (called prostheses) nowadays, and losing an arm or leg is not as bad as it sounds. People who have an arm or leg removed can still ski, hike, or drive a car (when they are old enough to get a driver's license!). There are even limbs specially designed for sports like running or basketball.

Doctors sometimes remove the bone with the tumor and replace it with bone from a donor. Substitute bones also are made from cobalt, chrome, or steel. This is called limb salvage. Chemotherapy (drugs that kill cancer cells) is always given to kids with Ewing's sarcoma since this type of cancer responds well to it. Radiation is used for children whose tumors cannot be completely removed with surgery.

This bone has been reconstructed.

Hodgkin's disease

Hodgkin's disease is a cancer of the lymph system. In the last chapter we talked about a whole series of vessels in your body that carry a fluid called lymph. Many places in these vessels have little nodes full of white blood cells. The spleen in your abdomen (to the left of your stomach) also is made of lymph tissue, just like lymph nodes. So, when you have Hodgkin's disease, cancer grows in these tissues.

Often, one of the first signs of the disease is swelling of the lymph nodes and the spleen. Sometimes children or teenagers think they are gaining weight when they have to get pants with a bigger waist because their spleen is getting bigger under the skin.

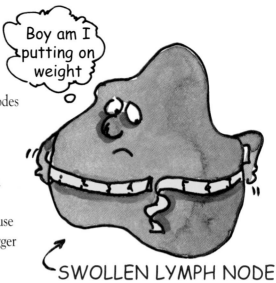

SWOLLEN LYMPH NODE

About 850 kids and teenagers in the U.S. get Hodgkin's disease every year. Not many children under 5 years old get this type of cancer. It's much more common in people over 10.

Treatment for Hodgkin's disease is based on many things. First, the doctor asks questions about fevers, night sweats, or weight loss. The doctor will do a physical examination to see if the spleen is too big or any lymph nodes are swollen and hard. X-rays are taken and an operation is done to remove lymph nodes inside the body. These are examined under a microscope. Your doctor will determine the appropriate treatment after considering all of the results from these tests.

Radiation works very well against this disease, so it is used for some children and teens. Chemotherapy is usually given as well. Years ago, every child or teenager with Hodgkin's disease had an operation to remove the spleen. Now, this is only done if absolutely necessary.

Leukemia

Your blood is full of different types of cells. The white blood cells (called WBCs) are your body's army to hunt down and get rid of foreign bacteria and viruses that can make you sick.

The bone marrow inside your hips, spine, and long bones makes a steady stream of new white blood cells to replace old ones. Baby white cells stay in the marrow while they mature into adult cells that can do the important job of protecting your body. Sometimes, some of the baby white cells, instead of growing up and doing their job, start to divide into more and more baby cells. Pretty soon, the marrow is full of cancerous baby white cells that don't work. This blood cancer is called leukemia.

When your bone marrow gets stuffed with baby white cells, it stops making normal white blood cells, red blood cells, and platelets. Without any grown up white blood cells to fight off illnesses, you start getting sick more often. Red blood cells carry oxygen that gives you energy. When the

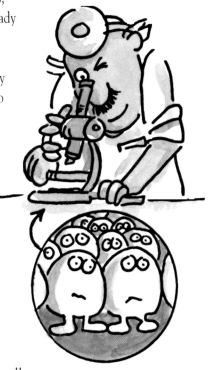

There are too many baby white cells in here!

number of red blood cells gets low, you feel tired and look pale. Without enough platelets, you bleed easily. If you bump your skin, you will get a big bruise. This is how kids usually get diagnosed with leukemia. They get sick a lot, are tired, look pale, and have lots of bruises.

Leukemia is the most common cancer in children less than 19 years old. The two main types of leukemia that kids get are acute lymphoblastic leukemia (ALL for short) and acute myelogenous leukemia (AML for short). Let's talk about ALL first.

ALL is cancer in a type of white blood cells called lymphocytes. About 75% percent of kids with leukemia have ALL—that's about 2,400 kids in the U.S every year. Kids of any age can get ALL, but it is most common in children ages 2 to 4.

ALL is very curable but it takes a lot of treatment. Girls are treated for over two years, and boys for over three. The main therapy for ALL is chemotherapy (drugs that kill cancer cells). Children whose ALL has spread to the brain or testes need radiation. A few other children at very high risk for relapse (when the disease comes back) need radiation to the brain as well and may need a bone marrow or stem cell transplant. Surgery is not needed to treat the disease, but it can be used to put a central line (catheter) in the chest so you won't get lots of needle pokes.

Acute myelogenous leukemia (AML) is cancer usually found in a type of white blood cell called a granulocyte. Approximately 500 kids are diagnosed in the U.S. with this disease each year Treatment for AML is intensive chemotherapy and sometimes bone marrow or stem cell transplant.

Neuroblastoma

Neuroblastoma is a cancer of the sympathetic nervous system—a network of nerves that carries messages from the brain to all parts of the body. Neuroblastoma usually starts in one of the adrenal glands which sit on top of each kidney. Sometimes neuroblastoma starts in other places in the abdomen, or the neck, chest, or pelvis. Because it's a big lump deep inside your body, it is often hard to diagnose.

Approximately 700 infants and young children in the U.S. get neuroblastoma every year. The average age at diagnosis is 2, but 25% of all cases are in babies under one year old.

Treatment for neuroblastoma depends on your age, where it is in your body, whether it has spread to other places inside your body, and how it looks under the microscope. Once the doctors have all this information, they decide on the best treatment. All kids with neuroblastoma have surgery, either to remove the whole tumor or to take a little piece to look at under the microscope. Most children with neuroblastoma also get chemotherapy (drugs that kill cancer cells), since it helps shrink the tumor and kill any little bits of it that have gone to other places in the body.

Radiation works very well against this disease, so many children get radiation as well. Sometimes treatment includes bone marrow or stem cell transplants.

Non-Hodgkin's lymphoma

Non-Hodgkin's lymphoma (also called NHL) is a cancer of the lymph system. This system is made up of lymph vessels throughout the body that carry a colorless liquid called lymph. Throughout this network, groups of small organs called lymph nodes, make and store white blood cells that fight infection.

Lymph tissue is found throughout the body, so NHL can be found in almost any organ or tissue such as the liver, bone marrow, or spleen. Doctors can tell Hodgkin's and non-Hodgkin's  lymphomas apart by looking at the cells under a microscope. Because they are cancers in different types of cells, different treatments are used.

The white cells that get cancer in non-Hodgkins lymphoma are called B cells or T cells. The three most common kinds of NHL in children are called lymphoblastic, small noncleaved cell lymphoma (Burkitt's and non-Burkitt's), and large cell lymphoma.

Approximately 800 children under the age of 20 in the U.S. are diagnosed with NHL every year. It is rare in very young children and 70% of all cases of childhood NHL occur in boys.

Treatment for NHL depends on where it is in your body, whether it has spread to other places inside your body, and how it looks under the microscope. Once the doctors have all this information, they decide on the best treatment. All kids with NHL are given chemotherapy (drugs that kill cancer cells) since it is so effective against this cancer.

Sometimes, children with NHL need radiation. Occasionally radiation is used if a tumor in the chest is making it hard for you to breathe or if a tumor is pressing on an important blood vessel. Also, if boys have tumors in their testes, they sometimes need radiation there. Surgery is needed to take a biopsy and to put a catheter in your chest so you won't need as many needle pokes.

Osteosarcoma

Osteosarcoma is cancer of the bone. It develops in baby bone cells that would have developed into healthy bone if something hadn't gone wrong. These cells keep dividing until a big lump forms in the bone. Osteosarcoma usually grows in the long bones of the leg, often right above the knee. Less common sites for these tumors are the upper arm close to the shoulder, the hip bones, and the skull.

About 400 young people are diagnosed in the United States every year with osteosarcoma. Most of these are teenagers, and it is more common in boys than girls.

In the last twenty years, treatment for osteosarcoma has changed and improved. The only option used to be removing the part of the body with the tumor (amputation). Now, doctors can do a test on the tumor to see what kind it is (biopsy) and then use a machine to take a picture of the inside of the body (CT scan) to see if the tumor has spread. Chemotherapy always is given since this type of cancer responds well to it.

All children or teens with osteosarcoma have surgery. Sometimes amputation is necessary. But, there are really great substitute limbs (called prostheses) nowadays. Once a young man with a prosthetic leg ran across Canada to raise money for cancer research.

Doctors sometimes remove the bone with the tumor and replace it with bone from a donor or a bone from elsewhere in the child's body. Substitute bones also are made from cobalt, chrome, or steel. This is called limb salvage. Radiation doesn't work as well on osteosarcoma so it is rarely used.

Retinoblastoma

Retinoblastoma is a tumor of the eye. It is usually diagnosed when parents or doctors notice that the pupil of the eye looks white when exposed to light. This is called "cat's eye reflex" and often is seen when a flash picture is taken.

About 300 children and adolescents under 19 years old in the U.S. get retinoblastoma each year. It is usually diagnosed in very young children, and may be present at birth. Although it may occur at any

If you need eye treatment, doctors will give you medicine so you won't feel a thing. Eye promise!

age, 95 percent of cases are diagnosed before the age of 5. Retinoblastoma is a disease that can be inherited from parents. Children with more than one tumor or a tumor in both eyes (usually the hereditary form) are usually diagnosed at a younger age than those with one tumor in only one eye (usually the non-hereditary form).

There are lots of ways to treat retinoblastoma. Your doctor will consider the number of tumors, the size of the tumors, and if they have spread outside the eye. Sometimes, the best treatment is removal of the eye (called enucleation). If your eye is removed, you get a fake eye that is painted to look just like your other one. If you have a blue eye with a dark rim, the eye artist paints your replacement eye to look exactly the same.

There are three ways to treat little tumors in the eye.

- Cryotherapy uses a probe that is really cold to get rid of the tumor.
- Thermotherapy uses extreme heat to destroy the tumor.
- Photocoagulation uses a laser that focuses light at the tumor. This stops the blood supply to the tumor to keep it from growing.

Doctors will give you medicine before you get any of these treatments so that you won't feel them.

Chemotherapy (drugs that kill cancer cells) also is used for many children with retinoblastoma. Some children with retinoblastoma also get radiation since these tumors are very sensitive to it. It is given from a big machine outside the body, or by putting little pieces of material that emit radiation into the tumor during an operation.

Rhabdomyosarcoma

Rhabdomyosarcoma is a cancer that arises from baby muscle cells. These cells, called rhabdomyoblasts, are supposed to grow up into healthy muscle cells. Instead, they start dividing out of control, and pretty soon they make a big lump instead of a nice muscle. Because you have muscles all over your body, rhabdomyosarcoma can grow in all sorts of different places. The most common areas they are found in children are the head, neck, vagina, bladder, arms, legs, and chest.

How to trick a new doctor...

Errr, Doc, how do you spell rhabdomyosarcoma?

About 350 children in the United States develop rhabdomyosarcoma every year. Most of these children (66%) are under 5 years old when the tumor is diagnosed.

Treatment for this cancer depends on where it is in your body, whether it has spread elsewhere in your body, and how it looks under the microscope. Once the doctors have all this information, they decide on the best treatment.

All kids with rhabdomyosarcoma have surgery, either to remove the whole tumor or to take a little piece to look at under the microscope. All children with rhabdomyosarcoma also get chemotherapy (drugs that kill cancer cells), since it helps shrink the tumor and kill any little bits of it that have gone to other places in the body. Some children also get radiation therapy to help get rid of the tumor.

Wilms' tumor

Wilms' tumor is a cancer of the kidney. You have two kidneys, each a little bit below your ribcage towards the back of your body. These organs are about the size of your fist, and are shaped like kidney beans. They filter out all of the useful parts of the fluids you drink, before sending the rest to the bladder as urine (pee). You then get rid of the urine when you go to the bathroom. Usually, a Wilms' tumor grows in only one kidney, but occasionally, tumors grow in both kidneys.

About 500 children in the United States get Wilms' tumor every year. It is most common in children under 5 years of age. Slightly more girls than boys get this disease.

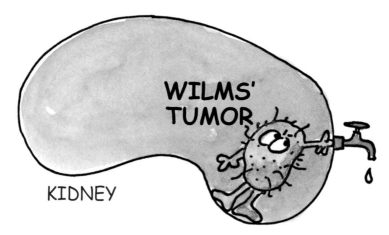

WILMS' TUMOR

KIDNEY

Treatment for Wilms' tumor depends on the size of the tumor, whether it is in one or both kidneys, how it looks under a microscope, and how old you are. Usually, but not always, the first treatment is an operation to remove the tumor and the kidney where it is growing. During the operation, the surgeon carefully examines the other kidney and he may remove a few of the lymph nodes in the area. Most children with Wilms' tumor get chemotherapy (drugs that kill cancer cells) because it is so effective against this type of cancer. However, some children with Wilms' tumor also need radiation.

Rare cancers

All of the above cancers are the most common ones that occur in kids. However, there are several rare cancers that very few children get. We'll talk about a few of them here.

Chronic myelocytic leukemia (CML) is pretty common in adults but rare in kids. In CML, grown up white cells called granulocytes get cancer. In the more common acute leukemias, baby white blood cells are the ones that get sick. Children or teens with CML get very big spleens and have a really high number of white blood cells in their blood. This disease is treated with chemotherapy (drugs that kill cancer cells) and a medicine called interferon alpha to slow it down. At the moment, the best chance for cure is a bone marrow transplant. However, there is a new drug, called Gleevec, which may become the recommended treatment. Your doctor will help you decide what is the best treatment for you.

Tumors in the liver are rare in children. The two that are sometimes seen are called hepatoblastoma and hepatocellular carcinoma. Most kids who are diagnosed with hepatoblastoma are younger than 3. Hepatocellular carcinoma shows up in children from birth to 4 and from 12 to 15. No one knows why they are most common during those years. Chemotherapy is usually used to shrink the tumor before surgery to remove it.

Melanoma is a cancer of the skin that is common in adults but sometimes grows in children or teens. Melanoma can spread from the skin to other parts of the body through your blood or lymph. Melanoma usually is removed during surgery. Sometimes chemotherapy or biological therapies also are used to treat it.

Nasopharyngeal carcinoma is a cancer in the area behind the nose and the top and back of the mouth. Children between the ages of 10 and 15 years get it most often. Doctors consider how big the tumor is and if it has spread to decide on the best treatment. High-dose radiation to the tumor is the usual treatment. Sometimes surgery also is used to remove any lymph nodes that didn't shrink during radiation. Occasionally, chemotherapy (drugs that kill cancer cells) also is necessary.

There are several rare soft tissue sarcomas that sometimes are diagnosed in children or teens. The ones found most often in children are: synovial sarcoma, fibrosarcoma, malignant peripheral nerve sheath tumor (also called neurofibrosarcoma or malignant schwannoma), and malignant fibrous histiocytoma. Treatment is usually surgery and sometimes radiation therapy. Chemotherapy is sometimes used to shrink large tumors before surgery to remove them.

 My Page for Pictures & Questions

Chapter 3

The Hospital

The first time most kids see the inside of a hospital is the day they are born. It is a happy event and they leave in a day or two with smiling parents. But most likely you don't remember that first visit. Moms and dads usually have lots of pictures, though.

You probably do remember the day you went to the hospital to learn more about your cancer, and to start treatment. That is a different kind of day than the day you were born. This time, your parents looked scared and maybe your mom or dad (or both) cried. And maybe that was scary for you.

The first day at the hospital might not be the best day. but it's the day you start to get rid of the cancer!

Even though going to the hospital isn't a time when lots of flashbulbs go off, it's still an important time. It's the day you start to get rid of the cancer.

That's a big day in your life, too. So big, that sometimes years later your family will have parties to celebrate the number of years you have been cancer-free. By that time you will know, just like oodles of kids before you, that you could and did handle everything that went on in the hospital. That's good to know, since you'll probably be spending some time in the hospital.

Let's see what goes on inside of hospitals. Let's talk about ways to deal with the things you'll experience there and maybe even have some fun.

The building

Hospitals are usually one huge building or a bunch of big buildings. Sometimes the whole hospital is just for taking care of kids. Other times, it has areas for both kids and adults. If it takes care of all people of all ages, you'll get a room on the children's floor. This doesn't mean the floor is made out of children! It just means that if you get off the elevator at the children's floor, you'll see lots of sick kids, but no sick adults. Lots of adults work there, though.

At the hospital, there is a special floor for kids only because kids are special!

FOR KIDS ONLY

The part of the hospital where kids stay is also called the "Peds floor." It doesn't have a floor that lots of kids "peed" on, even though it sounds that way from the name. "Peds" is short for "pediatrics" which is a big word that means kids.

There are lots of places in the hospital you might go while getting treated for your cancer. Children with cancer stay on the "ped's floor" for normal stuff—getting chemotherapy, treatment for fevers, and things like that. If children get really sick, sometimes they will stay in the Pediatric Intensive Care Unit (called the "PICU" or "pick-you" for short). In this part of the hospital, there are lots of nurses so sick kids have someone to watch over them full-time to help them get better faster.

If you get sick while you are at home, your parents may bring you to the emergency room—a place where doctors and nurses figure out what's wrong and decide whether you need to stay in the hospital or can go home.

There are many other places you may need to go in the hospital for treatment. Kids with cancer usually need x-rays, so they go to the radiology department. In that department, there are big machines that take pictures of your insides using sophisticated computers. They also have machines that give radiation (more on this in chapter 5). X-ray and radiation machines sometimes make noises, but they don't hurt.

Another place you might go is the clinic. Sometimes, when you are feeling better, you take pills at home and come into the hospital for short treatments. You won't have to stay overnight. Usually you spend a couple of hours in the clinic, and then you can go home. After your clinic visit, if you are lucky, you might go out for something to eat or go shopping for a toy or book.

Anytime you need to go to a new part of the hospital, ask your nurse to tell you all about it. That way, you'll know what to expect.

Your room

Some hospital rooms are small, with just a bed and a chair, while others have several beds. You could be in a room with your mom or dad, or in one with lots of kids and relatives. When you are feeling well, it's fun to have other kids around to play and talk with. On days when you feel rotten, peace and quiet may be better. Your parents (or whoever takes care of you) can ask if a private room is available if you want privacy.

Your hospital bed is different than the one you have at home. This one has gadgets on it. There are buttons that make the bed go up or down. Other buttons make the top of the bed (where your pillow is) go up while the bottom (where your feet go) stays flat. You can experiment with the buttons to see what your bed can do. Hospital beds also have bars on the sides. Some kids feel cozy since they know they can't roll out of bed. Other kids pretend they are in jail. Hospital beds are the same for kids and adults.

Most hospital rooms have TVs and some have VCRs. You'll get your

own remote, so there's no need to take turns with brothers or sisters. Your mom or dad may let you watch more TV at the hospital than they allow at home. It helps to bring tapes for the VCR, since the hospital might not have a lot to choose from. You can make a tape of your favorite movies or cartoons to bring to the hospital.

If you are only in the hospital for a day or two, it doesn't make sense to bring tons of stuff with you. But, if you'll be there for many days or weeks, decorating your room can make it feel more like home. Lots of kids bring posters to cover the walls. They put up pictures of their parents, grandparents, brothers, sisters, friends, and pets. You can tape get-well cards on the walls, around the windows, or hang them on strings from the ceiling. Balloons (mylar, not rubber) are fun to have bobbing around in the corner. A boom box and CDs can fill your room with the kind of music you like to hear. You may even have a phone next to the bed so you can talk to your friends. Like sharing a room at home, though, you need to be considerate of your roommate.

You can also bring some of your favorite things from home: crayons, markers, toys, board games, computer games, and books. Even on days you don't feel like reading, your mom or dad can read to you. If you try hard, you can pretend you are the character in the story, and go on an adventure in your mind.

Going to the bathroom

All hospital rooms have a bathroom. If you are feeling sick or tired, you can use a commode (a toilet seat next to your bed that you can't flush). If you can't get out of bed, you can use a bedpan (for girls or boys) or urinal (for boys) instead of going to the bathroom.

Hospital bathrooms usually have a shower and sometimes a bathtub. If you are hooked up to an IV, you can take a semi-bath using a washcloth, soap, and water instead of a shower. When you go to the bathroom, you'll have to take the IV pole with you.

Rooms have sinks, too, with special germ-killing soap. Doctors, nurses, and other hospital people should wash their hands before they touch you or anything else in your room. It helps you stay healthy to wash the germs down the drain.

Sleeping

Usually, you will sleep in the hospital bed and someone from your family can sleep on the pull out chair or cot in your room. If you sleep with a special stuffed animal or blanket at home, bring that to the hospital with you. It can make you feel better to snuggle up at night. Some children bring their own quilt or bedspread to sleep under at night.

Sleeping in a hospital is different from home in lots of ways. Hospital hallways have lights, so it never seems really dark. If lights bother you at night, your parents can get some night shades—those cloth goggles that some people wear on airplanes. Hospitals can be noisy places at night too, but if you stay there a lot you will probably get used to the noise. Often, nurses come in at night to take your blood pressure or temperature.

Getting around

When kids are feeling well, most of them use their feet to get around. They can walk, run, skip, or occasionally stroll. Some kids only have one foot, so they use a man-made leg (called a prosthesis) or they use a crutch in place of the foot. Kids on crutches get pretty fast. They run, walk, or stroll too. Kids attached to IV poles sometimes like to stand on the bottom part and let a friend or parent roll them down the hall. You have to be careful, though, since this makes doctors and nurses nervous.

Some kids who have just had surgery or are feeling weak from chemo or radiation get around in a wheelchair. You can decorate the wheelchair to look like a hot rod or a throne. Or tie an umbrella on it to make it look like a golf cart.

Some kids stay in bed until they are feeling more energetic. Even if you feel like staying in bed, you may need to go for treatments like radiation. Your nurse might pull you there in a wagon or let you ride a special hospital bike. Some places have little motorized carts to help bring children where they need to go. They might even push your whole bed down the hall. You can ask a nurse if there are any fun ways to move around in the hospital.

Eating

Eating in the hospital is a lot different than eating at home. Every day in the hospital you are given a menu to order your meals for the next day. If you like oatmeal, you can get it every morning. If you hate oatmeal, you never have to order it. Cafeteria workers push huge carts full of trays of food down the halls at breakfast, lunch, and dinner times.

Most hospital rooms have a kind of narrow table in them that swings over the top of the bed. Your tray sits on this table so you can

eat in bed. The tables are adjustable, so you can sit in a chair and lower the table to just the right height for you. Sometimes families spread a blanket on the floor and have a picnic together.

Sometimes kids in the hospital want to order pizza just like they do at home. The nurses and doctors can tell you if any nearby restaurants deliver hot food directly to hospital rooms. Maybe you could have a pizza party! Lots of hospitals have little kitchens where parents can cook or heat up your favorite foods right there.

You can also eat in the hospital cafeteria, but your mom or dad will have to pay for it. Cafeterias have lots of choices and you can pick out food that looks good to you. Chemotherapy drugs can make some things taste strange or yucky to you, so you may have to experiment to see what tastes good. Some hospital cafeterias have outdoor eating areas, so you can sit out in the sun on warm days. Sunshine on a bald head feels toasty warm—but don't forget the sunscreen!

Playing

Most children's hospitals have lots of fun things to do. They usually have a big playroom where only adults who like to have fun are allowed. This room has different names like "recreation therapy" or "child life room." It is stuffed full of paints, crayons, paper, dress up clothes, games, legos, books, and more.

On days when you don't feel like playing or your blood counts are low (and you could get sick if around any germs) the child life worker can bring stuff to your room to play with. Child life workers love to do fun things with kids while they are in the hospital. If you are bored, ask them for some fun ideas. If you don't feel like playing when she gets there, you can just sit and talk or watch TV instead.

Some hospitals have little libraries on wheels. People push them from room to room and you can borrow books as you do at your neighborhood library. You might find some good books that you haven't read before.

Ask your nurse if there is a playroom or pushcart library at your hospital.

Sometimes interesting people come to visit kids in hospitals. Don't be surprised to see clowns, famous people like sports stars, or maybe even Santa Claus drop in. Once, a visitor to the peds floor (called the Mischief Man) painted faces on the backs of every bald kid's head and the kids put their clothes on backwards. Everyone was laughing and had a great time.

Exploring the inside and the outside of the hospital can be fun. Ask your mom, dad, or child life worker if they will take you exploring. You can check out the lobby, the playroom, the roof (if there is a door to it), or the outside gardens. Some hospitals have a helicopter landing pad—you might be able to see a helicopter take off or land.

If you are tired, maybe you can get pushed around in a wheelchair to explore. Some kids like to dress up for these adventures by putting rub-on tattoos on their heads or streamers on their IV poles or wheelchair. Others just put on a coat and hat and look around.

You can have little parties in your room if your blood counts are high enough. Invite other kids in for popcorn and TV, or to play with dolls or toys. You can turn the lights out and bat around a glow-in-the-dark beach ball. Older kids sometimes play cards or watch movies together.

Finding nice people

Lots of nice people work in hospitals and take care of kids there. But in the beginning it seems like a lot of strangers. Let's talk about the different people you might meet in the hospital.

Hospitals are full of doctors. What you might not realize, though, is that many of them are student doctors. So, here's an explanation of the different types of doctors. When someone wants to become a doctor, they go to college for four years. After that, they go to four years of medical school. When they are in medical school, they are called "medical students." They sometimes work in the hospital and wear white coats. But, their nametag just has a name with no "Doctor" in front of it.

After medical school, people get more experience by doing several more years of work called a "residency." During this time, they are doctors, but new ones. Sometimes medical students, new doctors, and experienced doctors all roam around in big herds. They call this "doing rounds" but sometimes it seems more like a round up.

On days when you feel good, it's sometimes interesting to let all of these students and new doctors talk with you and practice doing examinations. But if you aren't feeling good, you and your parents can say "no" to student doctors.

There are also lots of nurses in hospitals. They come in all varieties too. Tall, short, smiling, laughing, quiet, and loud. Some are student nurses, some are registered nurses, and some are nurse practitioners. Registered nurses (RNs) are the ones who usually take care of you when you are in the hospital. They give medicines, start IVs, and

Your medical team

help out. Nurse practitioners have more training and sometimes do procedures like spinal taps. Lots of times they work in the clinic.

You can play germ police as much as you like.

Child life workers are the people who help you prepare for procedures. They explain to you about what is going to happen and help you find ways to cope. Child life workers might teach you how to take a trip in your imagination, or how to blow bubbles when getting blood drawn. They will answer questions and make mysterious things easier to understand. They make scary things less scary and everything easier to think and talk about. Plus, they are usually lots of fun!

There are many other people in hospital: social workers, recreation therapists, radiation therapists, cafeteria workers, and maintenance workers. It takes a lot of people working hard to keep a hospital ship shape and to care for everyone in it. If you ever wonder who some-one is, just ask him about his job. He will probably gladly explain what he does.

Nine-year-old Jamie used to have fun with the staff. He'd sneak up and tape little notes on their backs that said things like "Give Jamie in room #5 McDonalds for lunch" or "Go home, we're out of chemo." He got to know a lot people that way.

One thing that all the people in hospitals need to do is wash their hands a lot. Doctors, nurses, play therapists, maintenance men, and patients all need to wash their hands often to keep from spreading germs around. The last thing a sick person needs is to get a germ and get sicker! So, you can play germ police as much as you want when you are in the hospital. Part of that game is to remind every person who comes in the room to wash their hands before they touch you or any of your things. It will help you and all of the other people in the hospital stay well.

Part of the germ police game is to remind friends and even family members that they can't come to visit when they are sick. They will do you a favor by keeping their germs outside.

Getting to know people

One fun thing to do in the hospital is to think up interesting ways to get to know the people who work there. Here are a few ideas, but you can probably think of lots more.

First, you can ask lots of questions. A few things to ask are: "Do you have any kids?", "What kind of music do you like?", "What's the silliest thing you ever said to a kid?", "Do you have any pets and what are their names?" or "What hobbies do you have?"

You can also ask that they provide a service for you before they can take your blood pressure, temperature, or do an exam. For instance, you can put up a big poster and have markers handy. Ask each person who comes in the room to outline his or her hand on the poster and write their name inside of their hand. This will help you remember all of the different people who come in. Or you could have a guest book for each person to sign.

You could ask them to draw a funny picture for you or to sing their favorite song while they work. You can have a "No pokes without a joke" policy. Anyone who wants a blood sample needs to tell you a joke first. If they don't know one, say you'll tell them one today, but they need to bring one the next time they come. Here's a hospital joke:

Knock knock.
Who's there?
Orange.
Orange who?
Orange't you glad I've got good veins?

You could put a joke book on your bedside table to help out. A list of other things to bring to the hospital is in Appendix C, Hospital Packing List, at the back of the book.

All of these ideas are little ways to try to make your hospital days a bit brighter. But the truth is that some days you'll feel like telling jokes and playing with other kids, and some days you won't. Just tell your mom or dad how you feel, so they can make sure your day goes the best it can. Almost always, after bad days come more good days.

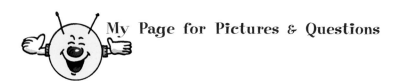 # My Page for Pictures & Questions

Chapter 4

Tests, tests, and more tests

T reatment for cancer can be quick (one operation) or slow (medicines for years). No matter how short or long the treatment, all kids with cancer have frequent tests to see where the cancer is in their bodies and to check on how well the medicines are working. After your treatment is finished, you will still get tests to make sure that the cancer is gone and to make sure that you are staying healthy.

Tests for kids with cancer are not the type of tests you get in school. They are not a way to see if you did your homework or if you remember how to do long division. Tests that doctors order are different ways to see how well parts of your body are working. This type of test is called a "procedure."

There are many different types of procedures that children and teens with cancer need. We'll talk about some of them in this chapter. But, you won't have all of these tests—probably just a few. You might want to just read about the tests that you need.

I WONDER IF THEY HAVE A CANDY EATING CONTEST?

Getting ready for a test

You don't need to study to get ready for a test in the hospital. You can ask lots of questions, though, so you know what to expect. It sometimes is scary if you don't know what is going to happen. Some of the people you can ask to explain about tests are:

• Child life specialists
• Nurses
• Doctors
• Social workers

They should explain what will happen, what it feels like, and where you will go to have the test. Maybe they can draw a picture or show you a video about it. Your parents will probably ask why you need the test and when you will get the results.

If you need to go to a special place for the test (like the radiation department for an MRI), see if you can get a tour first. For instance, some of the machines that do scans look like big, noisy donuts. But getting the scan doesn't hurt—you just have to lie very still inside a noisy donut. It helps to know these things before you go.

Here are some tips for making tests easier:
• Ask lots of questions so you understand what's going to happen.
• Make a plan. Some ideas are: take CDs to listen to, hold someone's hand (parent, brother, sister, nurse), take a video to watch, make a list of songs to sing, tell the doctor or technician jokes.
• Go on a trip in your mind to a favorite place. Imagine what you would see, hear, feel. If you like the beach, imagine the sound of

the waves lapping on shore, the gritty sand between your toes, the sun warm on your face. Build a sandcastle bit by bit. Go for a swim or ride a wave. Let your brother or sister bury you in sand and imagine the sun on your face and the rest of you cool under the sand. These types of trips in your mind make long tests go by faster.

• Use your plan to make the test go by quickly. Try not to delay things. Remember that the best test is the one that is finished!

• Do something fun afterwards, like cuddle with a parent, play a game, call a friend, or go out for a treat.

Common tests

We'll talk about the most common tests first. Almost all children and teens with cancer have these done fairly often:

• Physical exam
• Taking temperature
• Urine tests
• Vital signs
• X-rays
• Blood draws

After talking about those, we'll discuss other tests that only some children need. They are listed in alphabetical order so you can easily find a description of any test you are going to have.

These other tests are:

- Bone marrow aspiration
- Bone scan
- CT scan (computed tomography)
- Echocardiogram
- EKG (electrocardiogram)
- EEG (electroencephalogram)
- Hearing tests
- MRI (magnetic resonance imaging)
- Needle biopsy
- Pulmonary function tests (breathing tests)
- Spinal tap (lumbar puncture or LP)
- Ultrasound

If a test you need isn't in this chapter, ask the doctor, nurse, or child life worker to tell you all about it.

Physical exam

Physical exams are probably nothing new for you. You've most likely been going to the doctor ever since you were a baby. Before cancer, you went every once in a while. Now, you'll see doctors a lot. But doctors in hospitals do the same things that your doctor at home does.

- Asks how you feel
- Looks in your eyes, ears, and mouth
- Listens to your lungs and heart with a stethoscope
- Measures your weight and height
- Feels your tummy and other body parts

Be sure to tell the doctor if anything strange or new has happened. For instance, if you have a rash or pain, tell your doctor, nurse, and parents about it. You are the expert on your own body, so doctors depend on your information to keep you healthy.

Taking a temperature

Taking your temperature is easy and fast. The nurse or doctor puts a thermometer under your tongue, waits until the machine beeps, looks at the digital readout of your temperature, and writes it in your chart. Some hospitals use ear thermometers. They aim a small cone-shaped device at your eardrum, and it measures your temperature. These tests take less than a minute and don't hurt. Since fever is one of the first signs of infection, you'll have your temperature taken many times during treatment.

If you are having a hard time trying to pee in a cup, it helps to listen to running water.

Urine tests

Urine tests are used to test how well your kidneys are working. They also help doctors know if you have an infection in the parts of your body that urine flows through (kidneys, ureter, bladder, urethra). Some tumors (like neuroblastoma) give off substances that are found in urine. Nurses also sometimes measure how much urine you produce in a day, to make sure you don't get too dried out inside.

To get a urine test, your nurse will probably ask you to urinate (pee) into a plastic cup with your name on it. Or you can put a shallow plastic bucket (called a hat) under the toilet seat to catch the urine. This is probably the only time in your life you'll be allowed to pee in a hat! If you are having a hard time going in the cup or hat, it sometimes helps to listen to running water. So, try turning on the water in the sink.

Nurses test urine by putting a dipstick in it. The dipstick changes colors. Ask if you can watch the colors change if you're interested. You can learn a lot in hospitals if you watch what the doctors and nurses are doing and ask a lot of questions.

Vital signs

Taking vital signs is a complicated way to describe a few simple things that doctors and nurses check. These are:

- How fast your heart beats. Your doctor or nurse will put his fingers on your wrist and count the number of times your heart beats in a minute. Normal is from 62 to 130 times per minute.

- How many times you breathe in a minute. Normal is 18 to 22 times a minute. But if you have exercised or are scared, you will probably breathe a lot faster.
- What your temperature is. Normal is around 98.6 F or 37.0 C. If you have an infection, it may go up.
- What your blood pressure is. To do this the nurse puts a cuff around your arm and pumps it up for an arm hug. She'll let the air out slowly and measure your blood pressure while listening through a stethoscope. Results of blood pressure tests have a top number and a bottom number. The top number can be 90 to 115 and the bottom number 60 to 74. So, the nurse might say your blood pressure is "90 over 60."

Checking vital signs is done every so often when you are well, and a lot if you are feeling sick. Sometimes the nurses have to come during the middle of the night to check vital signs. After a while you'll sleep right through it.

X-rays

X-rays are pictures of the inside of your body. They aren't as clear as pictures you take with a camera. In fact, they look pretty gray and shadowy. But doctors who specialize in x-rays and other types of pictures taken with radiation can tell a lot from looking at an x-ray.

X-rays only take a couple of minutes and they don't hurt. The x-ray technician (person who runs the machine) will show you how to stand or where to lie down. Your parents can stay in the room if they wear a special covering full of lead (the lead is heavy). If your mother is pregnant, though, she'll have to wait right outside the door.

You may be asked to take a deep breath and hold it for a few seconds if they are doing a chest x-ray. The technician will press a button, the machine will make a small sound, and then you are done. You will probably need to wait a few minutes to make sure that the x-ray picture is good.

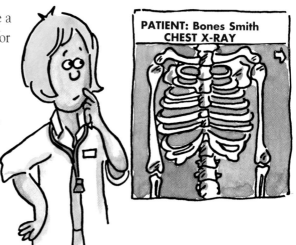

PATIENT: Bones Smith
CHEST X-RAY

Tips for x-rays:

- Don't wear clothes with metal (like jeans with a zipper). Sweatpants or drawstring pajamas will work better.
- Hold really still after the technician gets you in position.

Blood draws

Doctors need to check the blood of children with cancer a lot. There are many reasons. One is that chemotherapy can cause your bone marrow to slow down or stop making red blood cells, white blood cells, or platelets. Checking your blood helps the doctor decide if you need extra red cells to give you energy or platelets to help stop bleeding if you get a cut. If you don't have many white blood cells, you can get sick (like catch a cold) pretty easily. So your doctor might tell you to stay home from school for a few days.

Blood tests also can show if your liver and kidneys are healthy and working well or if you have certain kinds of infections. The laboratory measures lots of other chemicals to check on how treatment is affecting your body. Doctors have to keep a close watch on many things to make sure the treatment is getting rid of the cancer without hurting the rest of you too much.

There are four main ways to get blood out of your body to test it:

• From the tubing of the catheter in your chest (called a central venous line). You usually don't feel anything when blood is drawn out of the tubing.
• From the tubing attached to a PICC line in your arm.
• From an IV line. If you need an IV, often they will put it in, draw the blood, then hook it up so the medicine can flow in. Putting in an IV can hurt for a few seconds, but drawing the blood from the tubing doesn't.
• From a needle stick in your arm, hand, or finger. This can feel like a tiny stick or it can hurt a bit more if they have trouble finding a vein. Usually, it's easy to find veins in kids who were just diagnosed.

Tips to help with blood draws:

• Use EMLA cream or Numby stuff (anesthetic creams) on your skin before the poke. Cover with plastic or a watertight bandage. If it bothers you to have sticky tape pulled off, ask your mom or dad to buy some paper tape. This pulls off very easily, especially if you have turned back the ends to make a tab.
• For finger sticks, you can squirt some EMLA in a skinny balloon, then slip that on your finger an hour ahead of the finger poke. Your finger will look white and wrinkled when you

take off the balloon. To get lots of blood back in it, wrap it in a warm washcloth for a few minutes before the poke.

- Even if you don't use EMLA, wrapping your finger, hand, or elbow in a warm cloth before the poke sometimes helps.
- Try to distract yourself from the procedure. Some kids sing songs with their parents, hold a hand really hard, or use their mind to visit a favorite place. Others imagine the yummy ice cream or other treat they will get afterwards.
- Listen to music or blow bubbles.
- Read a book or watch a video.
- Tell the technician a lame joke. For example, "Why does a vampire always carry a red pen? So he can draw blood."

Other tests

The tests listed below are ones that only some kids need. You might need only one or several. It depends on what type of cancer you have and what type of treatment you need. You don't have to read through all of these unless you want to. They are listed alphabetically, so you can skim down to the description of any procedure you need. If you have some questions after reading these descriptions, write them down at the end of the chapter and ask your child life specialist, nurse, or doctor for answers before you go to get the test.

Bone marrow aspiration

The insides of your large bones (leg, hip) are filled with bone marrow. This is the factory that makes your red blood cells, white blood cells, and platelets. A bone marrow aspiration is a test to get a small sample of your marrow.

Years ago, children had bone marrow aspirations when they were awake. Now, almost all children are given medicine so they are asleep and feel no pain. You will wake up after the test and not even know you had it. You might be a little sore for a day or two, though.

Here is a description of what they do while you are asleep. The doctor or nurse practitioner will push a hollow needle into your hipbone. She will pull back on the needle plunger to suck out a small amount of the marrow. After she is done, she'll put a small bandage over the spot. The bone marrow is then tested to see if any cancer cells are hiding out there.

Bone scan

Bone scans are used to see if any cancer is in the bones or to see if the bones have been damaged in any way. Two hours before the test, you will get an injection through an IV of material that travels through the blood to the bones. You'll then go to the nuclear medicine department and will lie on a table. A huge machine will move back and forth above you. It makes a humming sound, but it never touches you and the scan does not hurt.

CT scan (computed tomography)

CT scans (also called CAT scans) use powerful computers and x-ray machines to take pictures of the inside of your body. The pictures are called slices, like slices of bread. The scanner takes dozens of these pictures of a cross section of your body. It does not hurt, though, and the machine never touches your body.

Before the scan, you may need to put some dye inside your body. You might drink it with juice, or they may inject it into your blood through an IV or your central line. Before you take the dye, make sure to tell the doctor or nurse if you have any allergies. You may not be allowed to eat for a few hours before the test.

The CT machine looks like a long donut with a hole in the middle. You will lie on a table that travels through the hole. You must hold very still so that the pictures aren't blurred. If you have a hard time holding still or get scared in closed up places, they can give you some medicine to help you relax and feel sleepy. Tell the people in the room how you are feeling before and during the test. There is a two-way intercom so you can use a normal voice to talk to the technician or your mom or dad.

Your mom or dad can stay in the room while you have the CT scan. Depending on how much of your body they need to scan, the scan can take just one minute or up to 30 minutes.

Tips for scans:
- Bring your own CDs to listen to. Most hospitals can play music in the machine during a scan, so you can listen to your favorite music while you get the scan.
- Squeeze your mother or father's hand or have them massage your legs or feet.
- Hold really still.
- Think of some of your favorite things. Go into all the details. You could think about your favorite baseball game, dance recital, or vacation.

Echocardiogram

Echocardiograms use sound waves to measure the amount of blood that leaves the heart each time it squeezes. This test does not hurt and it is interesting to watch. You will lie down on a table and the technician will put gel on a hand-sized instrument. The gel helps the instrument slide over your chest. Some hospitals warm the gel first (nice!) but others use it cold. As it slides over your chest, pictures of your heart pumping appear on a TV screen that you and your parents can watch. The technician can show you cool things about your heart and the blood flowing through it while you watch. The test only takes 10 or 15 minutes. The test does not hurt, but your chest will be a little slimy, so when the test is finished you can ask for a towel to rub off the gel.

EEG (electroencephalogram)

"Electro" means electric and "cephalo" refers to the head. An electroen- cephalogram measures the electrical activity in your brain. Did you know that you had elec- tricity in your head? Just like electricity runs a computer, a certain type of electricity helps run your brain.

The most common type of EEG is called a scalp EEG. A technician applies little pads to your scalp with gooey, easy-to-pull-off glue. Each pad is connected to a wire that goes to a machine. These wires are all different colors, so it looks like you have rainbow hair. EEGs take from 30 to 120 minutes, so it's a good idea to go to the bath- room before the test. In some cases, they do EEGs while you sleep at night.

EEGs don't hurt, but they can get pretty boring. Ask if you can bring a video to watch or music to listen to during the test. Perhaps you can read a book. If you have trouble holding still that long, your doctor might give you some medicine to help you relax.

EKG (electrocardiogram)

"Electro" means electric and "cardio" means heart. The electrocardiogram measures the electrical activity of your heart. You will probably have one of these done when you have your echocardiogram done.

Little pads with gel on the bottom are stuck on your chest. Each of these is attached to a wire that goes to a small machine. The machine measures the electrical activity of your heart for about 10 minutes. It doesn't hurt. Recordings of your heart's activity are printed out on a long strip of paper for your doctor to see. When the test is done, you'll need to pull the sticky pads off your chest and wipe off the gel.

Hearing tests

Some anti-cancer drugs and antibiotics can affect hearing, so you may need to have occasional hearing tests. One type of hearing test, called an audiogram, is given in a soundproof room. You go in with your mom, dad, or nurse. The person who gives the test will hand you earphones and explain that you should raise your hand every time you hear a sound or tone. Some of the sounds are loud, and some are very faint. This test only lasts about 30 minutes.

Another type of hearing test is called an auditory brainstem response (ABR). This checks the nerve (called the auditory nerve) that goes from your ear to your brain. This is an easy test that can be used on babies. You can even have it when you are asleep! The ABR uses a small speaker put against your ear that makes clicking noises. Electrodes on your head measure how the signal moves through the nerve.

MRI (magnetic resonance imaging)

An MRI machine uses magnets and computers to create lots of images of cross sections of your body. Imagine again that you are a loaf of bread and each slice is a picture of a part of your body. The difference is that each slice/picture from an MRI is very thin, and the machine generates many, many pictures for the doctors to study. Before the scan, you may need to have some dye put in through your catheter or IV. Make sure to tell the doctor if you have any allergies.

For an MRI scan, you lie on a table that slides into a big machine. Your parents can be in the room with you. The technician has a two-way speaker so he will talk with you during the test and you can tell him how you feel. Most MRIs take from 30 to 60 minutes so it's a good idea to go to the bathroom before the test. MRIs do not hurt.

Tips for MRIs:
- Wear earplugs. Most MRI machines make very loud, knocking noises.
- Bring a CD so you can listen to your favorite music in the machine if you don't want to wear earplugs.
- Tell the doctor if you have trouble holding still or are scared of closed in spaces or loud noises. He may give you medicine to help you relax.
- Hold your mother or father's hand or let them rub your feet or legs.
- Bring in a stuffed animal or toy to hold, as long as it doesn't have any metal on it.
- Stay very still during the test so the pictures aren't blurry.

Needle biopsy

Doctors often need a little piece of tumor to look at under a microscope to help diagnose what kind of cancer you have and to plan the best treatment. One way they get a sample of tumor is by a needle biopsy. Before the biopsy, you will be given medicine to help you fall asleep (anesthesia) so you won't feel any pain during the biopsy. Sometimes the doctor uses ultrasound or a CT scan to make sure the needle goes straight into the tumor. After the biopsy, the doctor will put a bandage over the spot where the needle went in.

After the biopsy, the bit of tumor is sent to a doctor called a pathologist, who will look at it under a microscope. You will probably have to lie quietly in bed for a few hours after the biopsy. It might help if your parents or brothers and sisters bring tapes to watch, a boom box with CDs, or games to play to help pass the time. You might be sore after a needle biopsy.

Pulmonary function tests

"Pulmonary" refers to lungs. So, pulmonary function tests check on how well your lungs are working. Usually, you will need to blow into a machine to see how much air you can breathe out. It's important to try to blow out as much air as you can. You'll have to blow into the machine several times. It doesn't hurt, but it's hard work! The technician will help you do your best. He or she might sound like a cheerleader. Family members can stay with you during this test.

Spinal tap (also called LP)

Your brain and spinal cord are surrounded by fluid called cerebrospinal fluid (CSF). All of the bones in your backbone protect the spinal cord and the fluid around it. If the doctors need to check for cancer cells in the CSF, or if they need to put medicine into it, they will do a spinal tap.

Most hospitals give children medicine so that they don't feel any pain during a spinal tap. To do the tap, you will curl up on your side in the shape of the letter "C". The doctor or nurse practitioner puts a needle between two of the bones near the bottom of your backbone, pulls a sample of fluid out and then puts medicine in if you need it. The needle is then taken out and a small bandage is put on the spot. When you wake up, you might feel nothing or you might be a little sore. Some older children and teens get headaches after spinal taps. For these children, it helps to lie flat after the spinal tap for one or two hours. Listening to books on tape can help pass the time.

Ultrasound

Ultrasound uses sound waves from a vibrating crystal that bounce off your inner organs, and you don't feel a thing. It is used to look at kidneys, pancreas, spleen, liver, or other organs. It is usually done in a dimly lit room and you can watch pictures of your insides on a TV screen. The technician will put gel on a device the size of your hand. It is rubbed back and forth on your belly. This test takes 15 to 60 minutes and it doesn't hurt. You just need to wipe off the gel when it's finished.

Looks like spaghetti to me.

Your insides!

You may have only a few of these tests during your treatment, or many. Ask lots of questions so that you and your family know what to expect. You, your family, and the people at the hospital are all on the same team—working to help you get better.

 **My Page for Pictures & Questions**

Chapter 5

Getting Rid of the Cancer

By the time cancer starts to cause symptoms in your body (bruises, tummy swelling, pale skin), it won't go away without treatment. However, doctors have many ways to get rid of cancer. They can operate to take out all or part of the cancer. They can aim radiation at the tumor to kill the cancer cells. Your doctors may give you medicines to destroy the cancer cells or prevent them from dividing and making new cells.

We'll talk in this chapter about the different ways that your doctors and nurses will help you become cancer-free.

Surgery

Surgery is when a doctor (surgeon) makes a cut through your skin to look inside your body. This is called an operation. You don't feel anything during the operation because a special doctor (anesthesiologist) gives you medicine to make you sleep through it.

Surgeons operate on children with cancer for lots of different reasons. Sometimes they only need to get a little piece of the tumor to figure out what kind it is and what the best treatment will be. Other times, they take out the whole tumor during the operation. Some children have an operation after they have radiation and chemotherapy to make sure that the entire tumor is gone. This is called a "second look" operation.

Many kids with cancer have an operation to put a catheter (central line) in the chest. You can read more about that a little later in this chapter.

Before the surgery

Before your operation, a child life specialist or nurse will explain it to you. She might show you on a stuffed animal what the scar will look like. She also will probably take you on a tour of the operating room or show you pictures of it. You can probably try on the mask that gives the sleepy medicine (called anesthesia). Anesthesia is sometimes a gas that you breathe in. It comes in different flavors like grape or bubble gum. Or, it might be given through your central line or IV. The doctor might give you pills or liquid to swallow. After you see the masks and the operating room, the child life specialist might take you to see the recovery room. This is where you will wake up after the surgery.

You might need x-rays or other tests in the week before your surgery. The doctor will tell you and your parents that you can't eat or drink for several hours before the operation. Ask the child life specialist, nurses, or the doctor any questions you have, because it helps to know what to expect.

The day of the operation

If your surgery is early in the morning, you probably won't be hungry. If it's later in the day, you might get hungry or thirsty. If you feel well, you can play a game with your parents, brothers, sisters, or a friend to make the time go more quickly. Cards, dominoes, or board games are some options.

When it's time for your operation, someone (a nurse or orderly) will push you to the operating room on a bed with wheels. You might get some medicine first to help you relax. Some kids like to bring a favorite stuffed animal, toy, or blanket to cuddle with. Kids who like to joke sometimes tape a little note or fake insect onto the part of their body that needs the operation.

The doctors and nurses in the operating room wear hats, gloves, gowns, and masks made out of colored paper (usually blue or green). They might look like aliens from a science fiction movie to you. All of those paper clothes are to keep germs from getting near you during the surgery. Underneath all of the paper are the same nice people who visit you in your hospital room. If you see the corners of their eyes crinkle, you'll know that they are smiling under their masks.

Most hospitals let parents stay until you are given the anesthesia. It's nice to get a hug and kiss before the operation and to know that you'll see them after the operation.

After the operation

When you wake up, you will have bandages and maybe some tubes in your body. Your nurse will explain what they are for and how long you will need them. If you feel any pain, tell the doctor or nurse and they will give you pain medicine to make you feel better. They might ask you to pick a picture of a face that matches how you feel (pain scale). Sometimes, they give you a little hand-held button to press that puts pain medicine in your IV line whenever you need it. You could give this machine a name if you want to, like "Pete the pain chaser" or whatever you want. Some kids like to hang a favorite stuffed toy or a picture of their dog or cat on the IV pole.

After the operation, the doctors will come talk to you and your parents to explain what they discovered and what's next in the treatment plan.

How do you feel?

Central lines

Many kids with cancer get a central line (also called catheter) put into a big vein in their chests. This invention is great. Years ago, every time a child needed medicine, a nurse would have to start a new IV. Now, with a central line, the medicine (or fluids or liquid food) is put in the central line and you don't need so many pokes.

There are lots of different names for central lines like Port-A-Cath,

Hickman, Medi-port and more. But, there are only two main types to choose from. One has a tube coming out of your chest with a cap on the end, and one is completely under the skin. Let's talk about the one with the tube first.

External catheter

The external catheter is a long skinny tube. One end is outside your body, and the other part goes under the skin of your chest, into a big vein in your chest or neck, then through the vein into the top part of your heart. When nurses need to draw blood or give you medicine, they do it from the end of the tube that hangs out of your chest. When you are not using the tube, it can be taped to your skin. Or you might like to wear a special snug undershirt to hold it tight against your chest.

A surgeon puts the external catheter in when you are asleep in the operating room. A nurse will teach you and your parents how to take care of it. You and your parents will learn to flush liquid through it every day or two and how to keep it clean on the outside. Lots of kids like this type of catheter because they almost never need any pokes. Everything is done through the tube. Some kids don't like it because it needs to be

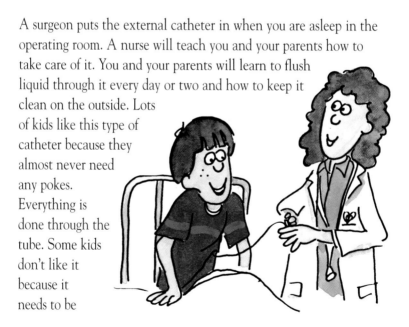

taped to their skin and they don't like having tape pulled off. Others don't like it because the tube shows up under tight clothes like bathing suits or thin tee shirts.

Subcutaneous port

The other main type of central line is called a subcutaneous (meaning "under the skin") port. It has a tube like the external catheter, but it doesn't come out of the body. Instead, it has a small metal chamber (about the size of a quarter but thicker) that is under the skin of your chest. A tube goes from the chamber under your skin, into a big blood vessel, and then to your heart. It's also put in when you are asleep in the operating room. A port only needs to be flushed once a month and your nurse will do that, not you or your parents.

There are two differences between the types of central lines. One is how you look: the external catheter has tubing coming out of your body and the port looks like a bump under the skin. The other is how they are used. To put medicine in the external catheter, the nurse injects it into the bottom of the tubing. The port needs to have a needle put through the skin into the chamber. This is called accessing. It doesn't hurt as much as starting an IV, but it is still a poke. Some kids don't mind it, and others use a cream anesthetic (EMLA, NUMBY stuff) or freezy spray (ethyl chloride) to numb the skin.

Choosing a catheter depends on lots of things. There is no right or wrong choice. Talk with your doctors, nurses, and parents

Freezy spray

about the pros and cons of each type. Think about how you feel about getting pokes, how you feel about the way you look, and how easy or hard it would be for your family to take care of an external catheter. You might tell the doctor about all of your hobbies or sports you enjoy to see if a catheter would affect them. For instance, some doctors don't want kids with external catheters to swim in public pools.

PICC lines

A peripherally inserted central catheter (usually called a PICC line) is also an option for some children with cancer. One end of a tube is put into a vein in your arm and then threaded up through veins until it gets to the top part of your heart. It takes a pretty long tube, since part of it is outside your arm and the rest in veins. This type of line can stay in for weeks or months. It needs to be kept clean and flushed just like the external catheter.

PICC lines are put in by nurses or oncologists, not surgeons. They will either give you medicine to make you sleepy, or will give you a shot to numb your arm so it won't hurt. You still will feel the tube moving up the veins of your arm and neck, though. You need to hold very still when they are putting in a PICC line. After it's in, they will take an x-ray to make sure the end is where it should be in your heart.

PICC lines are used for the same things as other central lines: medicines, blood transfusions, and liquid food. A nurse will take the cap off the end and attach an IV to it when they need to give you any of these things. When they don't need to use the PICC line, they flush it and put a cap on the end. It gets taped to your arm so it won't get tugged by accident.

There are different kinds of tapes that you can use for any of these lines. Paper tape isn't as sticky as the Tegaderm and other tapes used in hospitals. It comes off easier, too. Or, if you need to use any of the sticky tapes to keep your catheter in place, ask the nurses if they have adhesive dissolvers (like Detachol) you can try. Some kids don't mind having tape pulled off, but it makes other kids upset. If it bothers you, experiment with different tapes and dissolvers to see what is easiest for you.

In some cases, you won't get a choice of central line. Kids who need stem cell transplants or lots of chemotherapy usually have to have a special kind of external catheter.

One way to learn about the types of central lines is to talk with the other kids on the peds floor at the hospital. They might show you their catheters and tell you why they chose that kind. Plus, it's a good way to meet other kids on the floor. If you say you just got diagnosed and need to pick a catheter, the other kids will probably tell you what they think.

Chemotherapy

Chemotherapy ("chemo" meaning chemical and "therapy" meaning treatment) is a big word that means taking medicines to get rid of cancer. Kids usually just call it chemo. Years ago, doctors would give kids with cancer just one drug at a time. Then if the cancer came back, they would try a different drug. Now, doctors know that giving several drugs at once can often keep the cancer from coming back. So, usually kids with cancer get several different drugs at the same time.

Chemo is different from radiation and surgery. It can travel around the body to find cancer cells wherever they are hiding. There are lots of different ways to take chemo.

- By mouth. Many kinds of chemo come in pills or liquid to swallow. If the pill tastes bad (like prednisone) your mother or father can cut it in half and put it in a little gelatin capsule (size 3 or 4). Then you can put it in your mouth and wash it down with a

Let's get him!

Yikes! I'd better get out of here!

Chemo

CHAPTER 5: GETTING RID OF THE CANCER

tasty drink. Other kids like to mix pills with chocolate syrup, ice cream, oatmeal, or anything else that they like. If you don't like the taste of a liquid drug, there is no need to slurp it off a spoon. You can put the exact amount into a syringe (with no needle on it of course!) and squirt it into the back of your mouth. Then drink something that tastes good to wash it down.

- Through an IV, central line, or PICC line. Your doctor or nurse might give you chemo through an IV line, central line, or PICC line. Sometimes it only takes a few minutes to go in, and other times a computer pump puts just the right amount in over several hours. You will need to push the IV pole if you want to go for a walk while getting your chemo. Other times they might attach a small computer pump to your belt or put it in a backpack and you won't need the IV pole.

- During a spinal tap. Sometimes chemo needs to be put into the fluid that surrounds your brain and spinal cord. Usually, the doctor or nurse will put the medicine in while you are asleep during a spinal tap so you won't even know it is happening.

- Shots. Some kinds of chemo need to go just under the skin or into muscles, and the only way to get it there is through a shot. The good news is that they use really skinny needles for these shots. The bad news is that it still stings a little. You can use EMLA or other anesthetic cream an hour ahead to make the spot go to sleep, so you won't feel it. Or, you can ask the nurse (or whoever gives you the shot) to use freezy spray (ethyl chloride). This feels really cold but it makes shots sting less. Other kids like to hold an ice cube on the spot where they need the shot. And some kids take deep breaths, hold a hand, sing a song, or say, "One, two, three, shoot."

Chemotherapy can make you look or feel different than you usually do. When you stop taking the chemo, you'll go back to feeling and looking like your old self. The next chapter talks about side effects during chemo and ways to deal with them.

One, two, three!

Radiation

Radiation therapy aims a type of x-ray at parts of the body to kill cancer cells hiding there. Doctors aim radiation at the cancer or tumor, and are careful to avoid as many healthy cells as they can. The amount of radiation used is just enough to kill the cancer cells while trying not to hurt the healthy cells too much. Since your healthy cells are tougher than cancer cells, they might get sick from the radiation but then most get better.

Radiation is given in two ways:
- External (from a machine outside the body)
- Internal (put inside the body through a central line or an operation)

Some parents and children worry about radiation. But, once you know more about it, it's less scary. For one thing, it doesn't hurt. And usually, there are only a few short-term side effects like red skin, an upset stomach, and feeling tired. Radiation also can cause some side effects later, but that depends on your age, how much you get, and where in your body the radiation is aimed.

External radiation

External radiation comes from a big machine. On your first visit to the radiation department, you will meet the doctor (radiation oncologist) and the technician (radiation therapist), who gives the radiation. They will show you the machine and the table you lie on to get the radiation.

Most kids get radiation every weekday and get weekends off. You might need it for two weeks or up to six weeks. Each time you go it only takes a few minutes, so you'll have the rest of the day to do things you enjoy.

The most important thing about getting radiation is that you need to stay perfectly still. This helps the doctors aim the radiation at the exact spot where the cancer cells are located. To help you stay still, you will probably have some sort of device on the part of your body that needs radiation. For instance, if you need radiation to your head, you might have a mask made. They will put a warm piece of net over your face (it's easy to breath through) and it hardens in a few minutes. They then lift it off and cut out holes in it for your eyes, mouth, and nostrils. It only takes a few minutes to do. It feels odd but it doesn't hurt.

Radiation only takes a few minutes.

If you need a mask, ask the technician to make one of your hand first, so you'll know what it feels like. If your mom or dad reads you a story or you listen to some music, it makes the few minutes of mask making go by quickly. Every time you have radiation, you will lie on the table, have the mask put on, and then it will be attached to the table to hold your head perfectly still.

Other kinds of devices are molds made of your body to hold a leg or arm in place. Sometimes technicians use straps with the molds. The important thing is that you feel comfortable so you can stay still for the radiation treatment. When you are getting your masks or molds made, tell the technician how it feels. You could say, "Oh, this is so comfy!" or you could say, "The mold is pressing into my leg and it doesn't feel very good." By your sharing how it feels, the technician can make it as comfortable as possible. And no one knows how you feel, except you!

Sometimes, the technician needs to put tiny black or blue dots on your skin. They call these tattoos. But, they are not like the colorful tattoos that you probably have seen on some grown ups' skin. These are little dots the size of the period at the end of this sentence. These tattoos are made by putting a drop of India ink on the skin, then pricking with a pin. They look like tiny black freckles. They are very small but they are permanent. Other times they draw on you with a marker and tell you not to rub it with soap in the bathtub or shower.

Getting the radiation therapy is pretty easy. You go to the hospital every day (Monday through Friday with weekends off). The technician helps position you on the table. Your mom and dad (or whoever brings you) can give you a hug and then can wait right outside the room. The technician will make sure you are in the right position by measuring certain things and maybe shining a light down on you. Then he or she will leave the room and close the door.

Your parents and the technician can see you through a big window, and hear you through an

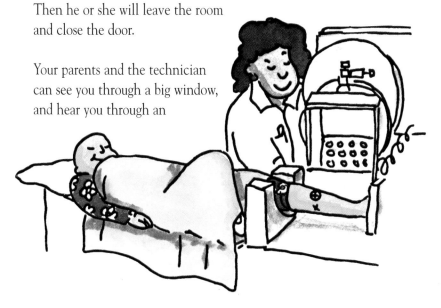

intercom. So, feel free to speak up if something is wrong. If not, just stay still for a few minutes.

The technician will turn on the machine, and it makes a buzzing noise. The machine moves around, but it will never touch you. You can't see or hear radiation but some kids get a funny taste in their mouths or smell something like rotten eggs. The treatment takes just a few minutes, once or twice a day. Each treatment is just like the first one, so you will know exactly what to expect after the first day. You have to stay perfectly still for those few minutes.

Tips for comfort during radiation treatment are:
• Lie on or get wrapped up in a blanket from home.
• Bring a stuffed animal or picture to hold.
• Put a sticker on the machine to look at.
• Bring a tape player with a story tape in it.
• Bring a boom box and CD to listen to (just don't sing along!)

Some children who are young or who have trouble staying very still get anesthesia for each radiation session. If you will have anesthesia, you won't be able to eat or drink for several hours before your radiation.

Internal radiation

Internal radiation is not used as often as the kind that comes from machines outside your body. Internal radiation means that little radioactive seeds or discs are put in or near your tumor. These deliver a continuous dose of radiation to the tumor. They are usually put in during an operation, and taken out several days later.

Internal radiation makes you radioactive for a little while. You'll need to stay in a room with plastic covers over the fixtures. Don't be scared by all the signs they put up to warn people. They are just to keep people from breezing into your room when they are not supposed to be there.

A parent can come into your room for only short periods each day. The rest of the time your mom, dad, or friends have to sit outside the door. This can be hard.

Here are some ideas on things to do:
- Your parents, brothers and sisters, or friends can sit outside the door and talk to you or read to you.
- You can make paper airplanes with notes written on them and fly them out the door.
- You could have spitball or water pistol fights.
- You could bat a badminton birdie back and forth with someone outside the room.
- You could sit and listen to music together, even though you are several feet apart.
- You can play videogames or watch TV or movies.
- You can email or talk on the phone to your friends.
- You can do artwork and tape it on your walls.
- You can make sculptures out of beeswax or clay and sit them all around the room.

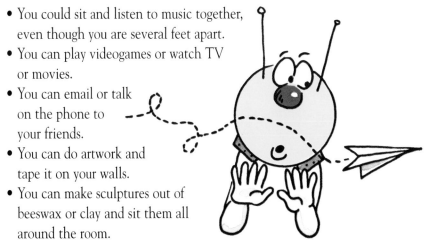

Once the implants come out, you aren't radioactive anymore and you can be with your family full time again.

Stem cell transplants

The center of your large bones is a very busy factory that works 24 hours a day to make new red blood cells, white blood cells, and platelets. This factory in your bones is called bone marrow. It is full of baby cells called stem cells. Red blood cells, white blood cells, and platelets grow from stem cells. The bone marrow is full of these baby stem cells, and some also float around in your blood.

Sometimes the best way to get rid of cancer is to kill off all the cancer cells with lots of chemo and radiation. This can stop your bone marrow from making new stem cells, so your doctor needs to give you new stem cells. This is called a transplant. Bone marrow, blood, or blood from an umbilical cord may provide these stem cells.

Bone marrow transplant

In a bone marrow transplant (also called a BMT), chemo and sometimes radiation is given in very high doses to kill tumor cells. This also kills the cells in your bone marrow. A bone marrow transplant gives you new bone marrow so that your factory reopens and starts to make new, healthy blood cells. There are two kinds of BMT: allogeneic and autologous.

Allogeneic bone marrow transplant

"Allo" means other. In this kind of transplant, you get bone marrow from someone else, called a donor. The donor's marrow needs to be a good match so that it will work well in your body. Since you get genes from both of your parents, your mother or father probably won't match. A brother or sister might, though. Or, your doctor might find a match from someone you never met before. Millions of people who are willing to share some bone marrow are listed on a computer database.

Once you have a match, you will get chemo and maybe radiation for several days. Then you will get the donated marrow. It comes in a bag, just like a blood transfusion. It goes through your central line and it doesn't hurt at all. It takes several weeks for the new marrow to settle into your bones and start up your factory again. During that time, you'll need to stay in the hospital to take medicines until you feel better.

During these weeks, it's easy to get sick with infections. Everyone (including all doctors, nurses, and family members) needs to wash their hands very carefully before they come into your room. You can be the germ police if you want. Ask everyone who comes in, "Did you scrub with soap?"

Some kids feel okay after a transplant, while others feel really sick. You might get sores in your mouth, throat, and intestines that make it hard to eat. You might feel really tired. You might look puffy if you have to take medicines like prednisone or dexamethasone. You might have other side effects, too. This is one type of treatment where you feel worse before you start to get better. You, your parents, and your doctor should talk over all of the things that might or might not happen, so you won't be surprised.

When your new bone marrow is working well and you start to feel better, you can go home.

Autologous bone marrow transplant

"Auto" means self. In this kind of transplant, some of your marrow is removed from your hipbones. Your doctor will give you an anes-

thetic to put you to sleep so you don't feel it when they remove the marrow. After you wake up, you might be a little sore for a day or two. Your doctor will freeze the marrow until it is time to give it back to you.

Healthy Red Blood Cells

You will get high doses of chemotherapy and maybe radiation to kill all of the cancer cells. This is called "conditioning." After that, they will thaw the bag of frozen marrow, and hang it on an IV pole. It will drip through your central line into your veins. It doesn't hurt.

Your bone marrow cells will go back to your marrow, and start making lots of healthy red blood cells, white blood cells, and platelets. Until that starts to happen, you are at risk for getting infections. So your family and doctors and nurses will take precautions (like washing their hands) so that they don't carry germs into your room. When your bone marrow starts making healthy cells, you'll feel better, and will be able to go home. Like other types of transplants, you usually feel worse before you start to get better.

Blood stem cell transplants

Your bone marrow is full of stem cells. Some of them float around in your blood, too. Stem cells are like baby cells, since they will grow and develop into all different kinds of cells. In a stem cell transplant, you will get some of your own stem cells back or ones from a donor (a person who gives cells to other people). If your mother is going to have a baby, sometimes her doctors save the blood in the umbilical cord after the baby is born. Babies don't need umbilical cords after they are born and the cord is chock full of stem cells. This is called a cord blood transplant.

The first step, if the stem cells will come from blood, is to give you or your donor medicines called growth factors. This makes your bone marrow work overtime to make lots of new stem cells. The marrow gets full of the baby blood cells and they spill out and float around in the blood. This makes it easier to collect them.

You or your donor will have the stem cells collected by a big machine. You'll have an IV in each arm or a catheter inserted in your leg. Blood is taken out of one and it flows through the machine that collects the stem cells. Then the blood goes back into you through the other IV or catheter. You may need to have this done several times to get

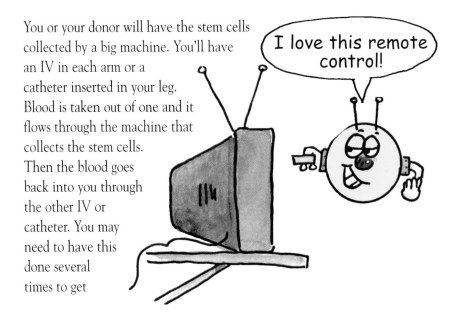

I love this remote control!

enough cells for your transplant. It helps to pass the time if you watch movies or listen to music you bring from home. Sometimes they will have a TV set in the room for you to watch.

The goal is to get rid of cancer...

After you have chemotherapy (and maybe radiation), the stem cells are put back into your blood through your central line. Sometimes, your doctor will recommend a series of stem cell transplants. These are called mini transplants or serial transplants. "Serial" means one after the other, not something you eat for breakfast.

Treatment is different for each child. Some breeze through and others have rough times. But the goal is the same for every child with cancer: to get rid of the cancer so you can be healthy again.

 My Page for Pictures & Questions

Chapter 6

Dealing with Side Effects

I t takes pretty powerful treatments to get rid of cancer. Radiation, surgery, chemotherapy, and transplants can have lots of side effects. Some are mild, like a rash that is easily treated. Other side effects can make you feel really tired for a while or change the way you look—like losing your hair. Some treatments affect the way you think or the way your body works.

This chapter describes a lot of the side effects that kids with cancer can get and ways to cope. It's divided into four parts: How you look, how you think, how your body works, and how you feel. Just remember, you won't get all of the problems described in this chapter. You might get only one or a few.

Bald is beautiful! I should know!

You can ask your doctor and nurse which side effects you may get based on the treatment you need. That way you can read about them and be prepared. The other thing to remember is that these side effects can sometimes be unpleasant, but doctors and nurses can do lots of things to help.

How you look

The next few pages talk about how treatment can affect the way you look.

Hair

Many types of chemotherapy cause hair to fall out. Here's why: Cancer cells divide a lot to make copies of themselves, so many chemo drugs target cells that are dividing. The problem is that some healthy cells divide a lot too. Hair cells, for instance. The chemo that kills dividing cancer cells can kill some dividing hair cells, too.

When you take chemotherapy, your hair may start to fall out. It can happen gradually. You might notice that more and more hair is on your hairbrush every day and your hair is looking pretty thin. Or you wake up one morning and most of your hair is on the pillow. Some kids lose hair all over their body—head, eyebrows, even the fine hair on their arms and legs. Others only lose the hair on their heads. And some never lose their hair; it just gets thin and wispy.

Radiation can also cause hair loss, but just in the places where the radiation is aimed. It also depends on the dose of radiation. The higher the dose, the more likely it is that you will lose some hair. If your whole head is irradiated with a relatively small dose (like for some kids with leukemia) you might not lose all of your hair. If your whole head is irradiated with a higher dose (like some kids with brain tumors), all of your hair will fall out. If you get a really high dose to a small area, the hair might not grow back. But, the bare spot might be in a place where you can grow hair near it to cover it up.

Hats are cool for covering bald heads!

Here are some things you can do if your hair starts to fall out:

- Don't use strong shampoos or a blow dryer. They might damage your hair more.
- Use a soft brush so it doesn't pull out more hair.
- Use a lint roller to clean up all the hairs that fall on your clothes or pillow.
- Get your head shaved. Then there is less to fall out. Some of your family members and friends might shave, too!
- Keep a bit of your hair in case you decide you want a wig. The wig maker will look at your hair to make sure you get the right color wig.
- Collect a bunch of cool hats, caps, scarves, or turbans to wear.
- Go bald—lots of people do—like Michael Jordan.

How you want to deal with your hair loss is up to you—not your parents, friends, or classmates. Some kids like to wear a hat at school and be bald at home. Others like to wear a wig all the time. Some kids like to have their friends decorate the back of their bald heads with drawings or rub on tattoos. Some girls like to wear stylish turbans when they dress up. Others like baseball caps. There are even hats with fake hair attached that look real! (Some places to get hats are listed in the Resources section in the back of the book).

One boy who liked to go fishing kept all of his hair in a big bag and used it to make fishing lures. They were called "Preston's Human Hair Flies." A local shop sold the lures to fishermen. Preston made some money and helped people catch a lot of fish.

Losing your hair is a pretty visible sign that you are being treated for cancer. Kids have many different feelings about it. So, it's natural that there are lots of different ways to deal with it. You may want to get ideas from your best friends or a special aunt or uncle or cousin or teacher. If you can't roam around to discuss this, email and telephone work just as well.

When you have made up your mind, tell your parents how you want to handle it. The way you choose is the right way for you. You might change your mind over time, too. In the beginning you might like to wear a hat and later you might like to go bald. Or vice versa. Whatever you decide is okay.

Skin and nails

Skin is another part of your body that has lots of dividing cells. Have you ever noticed little dry flakes coming off your skin? The flakes are old dead cells that have been replaced by fresh new cells. So, chemotherapy can cause skin problems because it affects the dividing cells in your skin. The most common skin problems are rashes, redness, itching, peeling, dry skin, or acne.

Some things you can do to prevent or treat skin problems are:

- Avoid taking really hot baths or showers since these can dry your skin more.
- Use a moisturizing soap.
- Rub on lots of moisturizer lotion if your skin is dry or itchy.
- Use sunscreen when you go out (SPF 30 or higher).

- If you are bald, wear a hat, wig, or scarf so you don't get a sunburned head.
- Use baby oil in your bath water.

It's a good idea to tell your doctor about red or itchy skin. If you scratch it too much, it can get infected. Your doctor might give you a prescription for a soothing lotion or cream that helps.

Chemotherapy also affects nails. The part of your nail that grows is right by the cuticles where the lighter half moon is. These rapidly dividing cells can die from the chemo. So, you might see a white band across the nail as it grows out. The nail might feel bumpy too. The white part will eventually get closer to the tip of your finger as the healthy nail grows behind it. It might break off or you can trim it with nail clippers. You could paint or decorate your nails until they are back to normal.

Your skin might get red and look sunburned from radiation. This only happens on the part of your body that got radiation. Ask the nurse or technician if they have any special creams or powders to make your skin feel better. Skin that got radiation will be sensitive to the sun for the rest of your life. So make sure to wear SPF 30 sunscreen whenever you go out in the sun.

Scars

Most kids with cancer finish treatment with some scars on their bodies. Some scars are little and hidden and some are big and more noticeable. For instance, most kids have small scars on their chests where a central line was put in and taken out. These scars are a straight line an inch or two long. Over time, they gradually fade and are often hard to notice. Some kids, especially those with dark skin, have skin that gets bigger scars, called keloids.

Other kids can have big scars from surgery to take out a tumor. If you had a brain or spinal cord tumor taken out, it can leave scar on your head or neck. Sometimes hair grows to cover it up and other times it doesn't. One girl who had a kidney taken out because of Wilms' tumor says she just doesn't wear bikinis anymore since one-piece bathing suits cover up the scar. Other people don't mind showing their scars—they are like a medal for beating the cancer.

People have all sorts of feelings about their scars and these feelings sometimes change as you grow older.

Size

The size of your body may change during treatment. You might get thinner or heavier. Or, you might stay the same.

Some kids lose weight because they feel nauseated and don't want to eat. Others find that the chemotherapy changes the way things taste. For instance, chocolate cake might taste bitter or meat might taste gross. Your sense of smell can affect how hungry you are, and often kids on chemo think a lot of things smell pretty bad. Some medicines affect your appetite, so even if things look and smell good, you just might not be hungry.

Those are the reasons you might not eat enough and may get thinner.

Gross. That hamburger smells like my dad's old jogging socks!

Here are the reasons you should try to eat healthy foods anyway. First, your body is fighting off cancer. Just like an army needs to be strong to win a battle, so do you. It helps your body heal if you eat healthy foods. Second, your body needs to break down all of the dead cancer cells into little pieces and get rid of them. That takes a lot of energy, and your energy comes from the food you eat. Third, your body needs to repair any healthy cells that the treatments damage. You need to eat good food to grow hair and heal from surgery and get taller.

If you have only a small appetite, it helps to get the most nutrition in the least food. You can cover mashed potatoes with butter. You can pour cream over oatmeal. Some kids eat ice cream for breakfast. Your mom can put nuts and fruits into muffins.

Try to nibble on healthy snacks all day instead of eating only three meals. Some snacks you could eat are:
- Fruit
- Burritos
- Celery with cheese or peanut butter
- Crackers with tuna salad or cheese

- Chips and bean dip
- Milkshakes
- Nuts
- Vegetables like carrots or broccoli with your favorite dip
- Yogurt (in a container or frozen)

You could make a list of foods that you like so your parents can buy them for you at the store. Making mealtimes fun helps, too. You can do things like use veggies, cheese, nuts, or raisins to make faces on the tops of casseroles or cereal. You can spread a tablecloth on the floor at home or the hospital and have an indoor picnic. Listening to music, eating in candlelight, or having a fun conversation at mealtimes helps, too. Eating as much good food as you can will help you feel better soon and you'll have more energy to play.

Other times during treatment, you may eat all the time. Medicines like prednisone or dexamethasone give kids huge appetites. They are hungry twenty-four hours a day and eat large amounts of food. Even little kids might eat three dinners or wake up in the middle of the night to go get more food. They wish they could live at a restaurant!

One boy carried a can of soup and can opener with him everywhere he went so he would always have some food handy. Others carry bags of snacks with them.

The medicines are doing their job but it can make you chubby. They can also cause your body to store lots of fluids, especially in your cheeks and tummy. If you see bald kids with plump cheeks and a big tummy in the hospital, they are probably taking prednisone or dexamethasone. Most of the time, doctors and parents let kids eat as much healthy food as they want. If you get too big, they might try to help you cut back on your eating a bit. Wearing pants with elastic waists (like sweat pants) might help you stay more comfortable.

Some parents keep two separate size wardrobes to fit the kid you are this month. However, in some places that have lots of kids in treatment and parent support groups, a clothes swap is possible. This way you can look really great no matter what size you are this week and it doesn't cost your parents a thing. If you have parties at your hospital for the kids on treatment or off treatment, you might arrange your own clothes swap and surprise your family. The good news is that you will gradually get back to your normal weight and appearance after you stop taking those medicines.

Size also means how tall you are. Often, kids on treatment don't grow as quickly as their friends. This may be because their body is too busy getting rid of the cancer and fixing damaged cells to grow. But, after treatment stops, most kids have a catch up growth spurt. You might shoot up several inches in the year after treatment ends. Talk to your doctor if you are worried about your height. If your cancer or treatment affects the part of your brain that controls growth, you may need some extra help to grow to your full height.

How you think

Most people take how they think for granted. Their brains just hum along, doing math problems or finding the right words to say. Having cancer and getting treatments can sometimes affect the way your brain works. That can be scary if you don't expect it.

Brains depend on many things to work well: good food, enough oxygen, the right amount of certain chemicals, and lots of other things. If any of these things get out of balance or damaged, your brain might work a bit differently.

Kids with brain tumors have the most problems with their brains—after all, a tumor is growing in there! How well their brain works depends on where the tumor is and how big it is. If you have a

Sometimes you feel extra sleepy or your thinking gets sort of fuzzy.

tumor in your brain, you might have trouble walking, talking, or seeing. Surgery or radiation to the brain can also affect how well it works. Sometimes, the problems get much better with time and healing. Your doctor or nurse can answer any questions you have about your brain tumor.

Sometimes kids with cancer have symptoms that require special medicines. Some of these medicines can stop the symptoms but change the way you think. Sometimes they make you feel extra sleepy or your thinking gets sort of fuzzy.

Kids with leukemia also get treatment to their brains. This is because leukemia cells like to hide out in the brain. Doctors give kids with leukemia medicine during spinal taps. This goes straight into the fluid that bathes the brain. They sometimes also get radiation to the brain. These treatments can make it harder to think clearly. You might find you have some trouble remembering things in school that used to be easy. Your thinking might feel a little sluggish. This happens to adults who take chemo. They call it "chemo brain."

Some kids with other kinds of cancer also get "chemo brain." It's annoying when it happens. The good news is that is usually goes away when treatment stops. Long-term problems with thinking can happen from medicines to the brain, radiation to the brain, or surgery to the brain. You and your parents can talk to the doctor about whether this is something that might happen after your treatment.

Usually, though, changes to the way you think come from being tired, full of medicines, and stressed. When treatment ends, you'll feel full of energy but empty of medicine. Your brain will have what it needs to work like it did before you got sick!

How your body works

Your body has many, many parts that work together so that you can run, think, play, and grow. Some types of treatment affect the way your body works. This section talks about low blood counts, transfusions, and movement.

Low blood counts

When you take chemotherapy, often your bone marrow gets tired and stops making cells. To check on this, doctors and nurses take samples of blood often. A technician looks at the blood under a microscope or puts it through a machine to measure how many white blood cells, red blood cells, and platelets you have in your blood.

If there aren't enough red cells floating around in your blood, then your body won't get the oxygen and the food it needs to work well. Having too few red cells (called anemia) can make you look pale and feel really tired. Luckily, if your red cell count is low, the doctors will order a transfusion. This comes in a plastic bag that is full of a red liquid.

If your bone marrow isn't making enough platelets, you can bleed easily. If you bump yourself you can get a really big bruise or your gums might bleed when you brush your teeth. Your nose might start bleeding and it just won't stop. To prevent these things, doctors order platelet transfusions if your platelet count is low. Platelets come in a bag full of a yellowish liquid.

When your white blood count is too low, you can't fight off germs so you can get sick easily. There aren't white cell transfusions, though. But there are medicines that can get the marrow to make more cells. Children with some types of cancer can get these to prevent low counts. But, most of the time you just have to stay in the hospital or at home till your white blood count goes back up. This means no school or playing with kids who are coughing or have runny noses. You can't go places with crowds of people. Too many germs!

When you get chemotherapy or radiation, it can seem as though your life is revolving around your blood counts. But, when your white blood count goes up, you can go back to your normal activities.

Transfusions

Have you ever wondered where the red cells and platelets used for transfusions come from? Adults donate blood for people who need it. These healthy people usually give one pint of blood at a time. The

blood is either used right away or kept cold in a special place called a blood bank.

The blood that adults donate is called "whole blood." It has many parts including red cells, white cells, platelets, and plasma. Kids with cancer usually only need one part of the blood at a time. So that nothing is wasted, most blood is divided into parts to help several people.

Red blood cell and platelet transfusions go into your body the same way—through a long narrow plastic tube attached to your IV, central line, or PICC line. Your nurse will hang the plastic bag upside down on a tall pole. She will check to see that your name is on the bag and that it is the right blood type. Then she will attach the long tube to the IV in your arm or hand (or your central line), and the cells will drip into your vein. It takes about 2 to 4 hours to get a red blood cell transfusion. Platelet transfusions usually take less than an hour. Most kids watch TV, play videogames, or read to pass the time. If you are very tired, you could listen to music or sleep in bed.

Most of the time, transfusions go well and kids just feel better afterwards. Every once in a while, though, your body can have a reaction to the blood or platelets you are getting. You or your parent should let the nurse know if you get any of these symptoms:

• Skin rash (redness)
• Itching
• Trouble breathing
• Fever
• Back pain

Luckily, transfusion reactions don't happen very often. But it helps to know what to watch for, just in case.

If I had any blood. I would donate it!

Most hospitals don't let parents or aunts and uncles donate blood for you. But, they can donate to the blood bank to replace what you use. That way, other children who need blood will have a steady supply. Plus, family members usually feel better if they can help in some way. So, donating blood helps everyone.

Movement

How fast you move and how coordinated you are can be affected by treatment. Some medicines, like vincristine, affect muscles and nerves. You might notice that your feet look or feel floppy. You can check this by trying to lift up the front of your foot. It it's hard to do, you have a common side effect of vincristine called "foot drop." It makes it difficult to run fast or go up stairs. Sometimes, if the foot drop gets very bad, the doctors might lower the dose of the medicine and/or send you to physical therapy.

Vincristine, and some other medicines, can also make your muscles weak. Things that were easy for you to do before get much harder. It can be mild or really noticeable. For instance, you might have a hard time standing back up after sitting on the floor for a while. Foot drop and muscle weakness usually go away gradually after treatment ends.

Some kids get these side effects from chemo, but others don't. Lots of kids play soccer, basketball, or other sports all through treatment.

Moving also can be affected if you need surgery that removes muscles and/or bones. Going to physical therapy or occupational therapy as soon as you are able after surgery can help you regain as much strength and coordination as possible.

Children who have brain tumors sometimes have problems moving. Depending on where the tumor is located, they might lose strength or control over part of the body. For instance, your right side might

be weak but your left side is fine. Or your arms might work well but your fingers don't. If these things are happening to you, ask your doctor or nurses if there is anything you can do to get some of your strength back. They might have some great suggestions.

How you feel

Surgery, medicines, and radiation can all affect the way you feel. This section talks about a few of the side effects that affect the way you feel.

Nausea and vomiting

Nausea means feeling like you need to throw up. Vomiting means throwing up. Many of the medicines you'll need might make you feel sick or vomit. Some medicines make you sick right away; others don't until you've taken several doses.

Years ago, there weren't good medicines to help with nausea and vomiting. Kids taking chemo just kept a bucket next to the bed and threw up a lot. Now, it's different. Medicines like ondansetron or granisetron can often make the vomiting stop completely. There are other things you can do to prevent nausea, too.

Here are a few ideas:
- Take medicines for nausea when the doctor tells you to. They work better if they are taken before you start to vomit.
- Try to stay away from smells that make you feel sick. Close your bedroom door or open a window if your parent is cooking and you don't like the smell.
- Eating dry foods like crackers or pretzels can help to settle your stomach.

- Bland foods like toast, soup, or potatoes are easy on the stomach. Spicy food can make nausea or vomiting worse.
- Chewing gum or sucking on Popsicles helps sometimes.
- Drink lots of liquids. If the smell bothers you, use a covered cup with a straw to drink.

Diarrhea

Diarrhea is when bowel movements (poop) are more liquid than solid. Instead of one or two bowel movements a day, you can have many. Diarrhea is uncomfortable, can make your bottom sore, and can make your body too dry inside.

Stay away from smells that make you sick!

Lots of things can cause diarrhea in kids getting treated for cancer. The most common are damage to cells lining the intestines from chemotherapy, infections, and some antinausea drugs. Having diarrhea is no fun, but there are many things you can do to help clear it up.

- Drink lots of liquids. Really hot or cold drinks can give you cramps if you have diarrhea, so drink water, juices, or Gatorade at room temperature.
- Your parents should describe the diarrhea to the doctor to see if you need medicine to treat it. It's nothing to be embarrassed about. Doctors who care for kids with cancer talk about diarrhea all the time! Make sure to only take the types of medicine the doctor recommends.

- Greasy, fatty, spicy, or sweet foods make diarrhea worse. So, try to avoid take-out fried chicken or greasy French fries. Fruits, nuts, beans, and raw vegetables also make diarrhea worse.
- Foods that help are bananas, white rice, noodles, applesauce, white toast, creamed cereals, cottage cheese, fish, and baked chicken without the skin.
- Keep your bottom clean and dry. If it gets sore, ask the doctor what type of medicine to use.

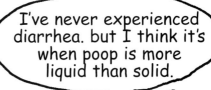

I've never experienced diarrhea. but I think it's when poop is more liquid than solid.

Constipation

Constipation is the opposite problem from diarrhea: you have too few bowel movements and the ones you do have are dry and hard. Constipation happens when the normal movement of food through the intestines slows down. Lots of things cause this: medicines, vomiting, and pain medications are just a few examples. Preventing constipation is easier than treating it after it happens.

Some things you can do to prevent it are:
- Drink lots of liquids.
- Get as much exercise as you can.
- Eat lots of foods with fiber like fruits, nuts, beans, whole wheat breads, and raw vegetables.
- If your doctor tells you to take a stool softener (medicine to

prevent hard poops), take it! The doctors know that certain medicines (like vincristine) almost always cause constipation, so they order medicines to help keep your bowel movements soft and comfortable.

Fatigue

Fatigue means being tired all the time. This happens sometimes when you take medicines for cancer or after you've had surgery. You might be too tired to get out of bed or off the couch.

If you got radiation to the brain, you might get really tired a few weeks afterwards. This sleepy time can make you sleep most of the day for several days. But, the sleepiness gradually goes away and you'll start sleeping just at nights instead of all day long.

If there is a specific reason for being tired—like not enough red blood cells—the doctors can fix it by giving you a transfusion of red blood cells. After you have a transfusion, you might feel energetic enough to go out and play. Other times, the tiredness can't be fixed. It's just your body's way of telling you to rest. All of your energy is probably going into getting rid of cancer cells and fixing damaged cells.

Here are things you can do when you are really tired:

- Read a book or a magazine
- Watch TV or videos
- Play computer games
- Do crossword puzzles
- Play dominoes or cards
- Listen to music
- Talk on the phone or send emails to friends
- Do art projects
- Cuddle up with your dog or cat
- Take a lot of naps

Fatigue comes and goes during treatment. Doing something fun can make the time seem to pass by faster.

Teeth and mouth

Radiation and chemotherapy can cause problems in your mouth. One thing that happens sometimes is that you don't make as much spit as you used to. You might never have thought about it, but spit serves a good purpose. It keeps your mouth moist and helps keep your teeth clean. It also starts the digestion of your food.

Dry mouth.

If you don't have enough spit, your mouth can feel really dry. It can also make your teeth look and feel pretty dirty. Drinking a lot of liquids can help. Most kids with cancer go to the dentist every three months to get their teeth cleaned and checked. If you have a central line in your chest, your doctor should give you antibiotics every time you have your teeth cleaned.

You also can get mouth sores from some types of chemotherapy. Mouth sores are like bad canker sores inside your mouth. These can hurt and make eating hard. Most kids find that it is easier to eat soft foods if they have mouth sores. Your parents can put food in the blender so that you can sip it through a straw. If you get mouth sores, your doctor might write a prescription for medicine to swish around in your mouth. They have anesthetics in them to put your mouth cells to sleep so they don't hurt. One type is called "Magic Mouthwash" and it helps a lot.

Pets

You might think its odd to put pets in the "How you Feel" section. Think about it this way. Do you feel better when you hug your dog in the mornings? Do you relax when you watch your fish swim around in their tank? Do you have a bird that sings in its cage or a hamster that makes you laugh? Pets can really make children and grownups feel better.

Parents sometimes worry about keeping pets if their child has cancer. But, with a few simple precautions, you can continue to enjoy your pet's company while you take your medicines.

- Your pet should have all its shots.
- Your pet should not have worms, fleas, or ticks.
- Don't play in the kitty litter box (ugh!) or in the place where your pet goes to the bathroom outside.
- Only have gentle pets—not ones that bite or scratch.

Pets are great helpers and healers. One boy always felt cold on the day he came back from getting treatment. On that night, and no other night, his dog would pull the covers up on him and sleep on his feet. Actually, it was a BIG dog so its head slept on the boy's feet, and the rest of the dog's body stayed along his side.

Four-year-old Kathryn had two big German shepherds. The medicine made it hard for her to keep her balance when she walked. So, when she got out of bed, the dogs would get on either side of her and walk with her so she didn't fall down.

Dogs and cats can be very smart about their owners. Do you sometimes think that you are the pet and your dog or cat is the owner?

Emotions

Emotions are how you feel. And having cancer can make you feel things you never did before. You might be really mad or extra sad. You might miss your brothers and sisters when you're in the hospital or be jealous because they can play outside and you can't. It can be scary if your parents cry or whisper to your other relatives and you

don't know what they are saying. You might
feel angry, scared, sad, lonely, or worried if one of
your friends in the hospital gets sicker. You will probably feel lots of
strong emotions during treatment. So will your parents and sisters
and brothers.

There are lots of good ways to deal with strong feelings. One is to
draw pictures of how you feel. If you are angry at the cancer, draw a
picture of the cells and what you would like to do to them (hit them
with a hammer, cut them up with scissors, throw them out the window). You also can make an angry list of all the things you wish you
could do like kick the wall, hit your brother, or lock the door so no
one can come take your blood anymore. Even though you can't do
these things, sometimes it helps you feel better to think about them.

But there are lots of other ways to deal with all the strong feelings
without hurting anyone's body or feelings. Talk to your parents and
let them know when you have some screamies to get out.

Here are some things kids do to feel better:
• Have a special room (like in the shower) or place (like the
  woods nearby) where you can scream as loud as you can for as
  long as you want.

- Punch and kick a punching bag.
- Rip up paper or wad it up and throw it around the room.
- Get a hammer and hammer nails into wood.
- Go outside and kick a soccer ball against a fence.
- Pound clay.
- Cry whenever you feel like it.

Exercise helps sometimes. If you are really angry, running fast or playing basketball might make you feel a bit better. If you are really happy, jumping up and down or riding your bike around outside feels good.

Talking helps, too. You can tell your parents, friends, or relatives how you feel. Lots of children with cancer talk to a psychologist or counselor (at the hospital or at home) about how they are feeling. Some kids call their counselor a "feelings doctor." The great thing is that they usually have lots of toys to play with and things to do to help you understand your emotions. It is usually fun to go to these appointments and you feel much better afterwards.

Sometimes medicines can change the way you feel. For instance, prednisone and dexamethasone can make you feel giddy and silly. You might laugh a lot and talk nonstop. Other times, those medicines make kids feel really angry. You might scream at people you love or even throw things. You might argue about everything. And, you can't help it. Some parents call prednisone "dreadnisone" because of these side effects.

Some medicines can give you nightmares, too. That can be scary or upsetting. It's hard for your parents, too. Try to remember these three things if the medicines make you feel like a different person than you are:

- It's the medicine affecting your brain that causes these outbursts. You are not doing it on purpose.
- It goes away when you stop taking the medicines. Then, you'll feel like yourself again.
- Be sure to tell the doctor, nurses, and counselor if certain medicines affect the way you feel or act. They might be able to help.

Having cancer is hard to deal with and everyone who gets it (children or grownups) has strong feelings about it. You can write or draw pictures about your feelings in the journal at the back of this book if you want to. Or you can talk to your counselor or favorite relative. You will learn a lot about emotions as you go through treatment.

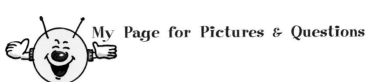

My Page for Pictures & Questions

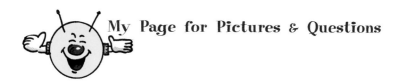

My Page for Pictures & Questions

Chapter 7

Family & Friends

When you get sick, you usually find out how many people care about you. It's pretty amazing how many people you are connected to, when you think about it. You have your parents, your brothers and sisters, your aunts, uncles, and cousins. You have your best friends, your neighborhood friends, and your school friends. You might go to church or temple or mosque and know lots of people there. You might dance or do karate or play sports. You'll know many kids and adults from these activities. So lots of people will be shocked at first to hear about your cancer.

Some kinds of news can be scary until you learn about it and get used to it. Cancer's like that, too.

Here's one way to think about it. Have you ever been on a boat in the waves? It feels very odd and unsettling at first. The surface under your feet isn't steady. You feel a little off balance and don't know how to adjust. You might even throw up. But, after a while, it seems perfectly normal. You'll probably feel really comfortable running up and down the deck and maybe helping with the sails or the motor. But it doesn't happen all at once; you need to get used to it.

Your family and friends need to get used to the idea that you have cancer. They will probably have a lot of feelings about it, just like you do. It might feel a little strange and uncomfortable at first. But, with time and good information, they will adjust, just as you will.

Parents

Having cancer is hard for you and it's hard for your parents, too. Parents usually have a dream in their minds about how life is supposed to be. They expect that their children will be healthy and happy, and that they will be able to take care of whatever little things happen. Parents think that they will be able to protect their children from scary things or pain. But, cancer can change that dream.

Even if you have been sick for a while, it's still a big shock for your parents to hear that you have cancer. Parents react in different ways. Some parents cry and some just seem sad and get very quiet. Sometimes parents have a hard time believing it. It's almost like they didn't hear it. They might say out loud that it's just not fair. One thing is for sure, though, they probably aren't acting like their normal selves.

Most parents want to pick you up and run away. But they don't, since their job is to take care of you. And they know, deep down, that that means bringing you to the doctor or hospital for your treatments.

Just like getting used to being on a boat, parents take a little while to get used to dealing with cancer. They have to take you to a big hospital where they probably don't know anybody. They have to get used to doctors and procedures and the new big words. They have to figure out a way to become a team with the doctors and nurses. And you are a part of the team. It takes some time to figure all of these things out.

Here are some things you might see your parents do to get the team working together:
- Learn all the players. Parents know that they are on the team and you are on the team. They need to figure out which doctor is the coach and which nurse practitioner

is the manager. They might write down the names of the team members. If you want to know who is on the team, you or your parents can ask team members to sign their names on the page at the end of this chapter. This might help your parents know what you are interested in learning about.

- Ask lots of questions and share the answers with you. You can write down your questions at the end of each chapter in this book so that you don't forget them later. That way, your parents will know what things you want to know about and what things you don't.
- Talk with you about what works best for you. For instance, if you need blood drawn, your parents can help you decide how you want to have it done. One boy holds his earlobe with one hand and his father's hand with the other. A girl likes to pick songs to sing with her mom. Talking over team strategy helps.
- Do things the way you did them at home. Your parents can bring in your bed covers and favorite toys. They can read the same books at bedtime and tuck you in the same way. This can make you feel safe and comfy.
- Decide that even though the side effects of medicines can be unpleasant, that the medicines are part of the team to make you get well.
- If the team is not working well together, your parents can call a team meeting. Doctors and nurses have meetings with families all of the time. All of you can brainstorm ways for the team to work together better.

Parents might also do a lot of things that are hard to understand. If you aren't sure why your parents are doing something, you can ask them. It takes awhile for some parents to figure out how to explain things.

There are lots of things parents might do that can help the family:

- Exercise. If your mom likes to swim, she might see if the hospital has a pool that she can use. If your dad like to run, he can explore the inside and outside of the hospital to find good places. If they are worried about leaving you alone in the room, they can have someone in your family or someone you like at the hospital come to stay with you for a little while.
- Eat right. Family and friends can bring nutritious food from home. Eating fruits and veggies rather than burgers and fries every day can make everyone feel a little bit better.
- Include your brothers and sisters. Brothers and sisters need to know what is happening to you and what will happen to them. It might help to let them come to the hospital. It might help you, too, to see your brothers and sisters. Your parents might ask them where they want to stay when you are in the hospital. More is written about this later in this chapter.

- Decide that the goal of the team is to get rid of the cancer and work towards that.

Brothers and sisters

Brothers and sisters are the people you've known all your life. You play with them and also fight with them. You might share a room or a bicycle or the same color hair. They will have lots of the same strong feelings that you do about the cancer and how it affects your family. Things can be pretty wonderful and also complicated with your brothers and sisters when you have cancer.

One of the first things that happens after you find out you have cancer is that one or both parents bring you to the hospital. Brothers and sisters are often left at home with grandparents or baby sitters. Or they might go stay at a friend's house. Imagine how you'd feel if you saw your parents crying and leaving to go to a hospital you've never heard of. You might be worried and scared. Depending on how old you were, you might even think your parents wouldn't come back. If you're a little older, you might understand that cancer is pretty serious, and you could get really scared. Some very young brothers and sisters think the parents and child with cancer are going off to do something fun.

Now imagine how you'd feel when you saw your parents come back loaded down with presents. And they aren't for you! Imagine if all the neighbors and teachers and kids in school kept asking about your sick brother. And no one asks how you feel.

Brothers and sisters of kids with cancer have a tough time. They get left behind a lot. They don't get presents and attention. They miss their parents when they are in the hospital with you. They worry about you—especially when you come home sick and bald. Or, if you come home feeling well with a bunch of big pretty balloons, they might feel really jealous and think you were off having fun. So, they might feel left out and angry too. They miss the way things used to be. They miss you and the things you used to do together.

They might not feel comfortable telling your parents how sad or scared or jealous they feel. Even if they do, your parents might not feel too sympathetic. They might tell the brothers and sisters that they need to "be strong" or "stop complaining." Or they might give the brothers and sisters a hug, but then go back to taking care of you.

Parents need to pay a lot of attention to you. They need to give you medicines and take your temperature and bring you to the hospital. Even when everyone in the family understands that, it is still hard.

You might miss your brothers and sisters, too. You might even feel sad about how hard things are for them. So what can you do to feel closer to your brothers and sisters?

Here are some ideas:

- Share the gifts you get. Six-year-old Matthew wouldn't open any gifts until he got home from the hospital. He would dump them all on the floor and let his older brother and sister pick the ones they wanted.
- Tell them what goes on at the hospital. They might imagine things that don't really happen. Like they might think you are locked up in a prison cell. Or they might think it's just a big party they weren't invited to. When you are in the hospital, you can call them on the phone or write notes to send home.
- Ask them to come to the hospital or doctor's office to keep you company. One girl always held her brother's hand when she had

What about us...

her blood drawn. He would tell her a story and it really
helped her.
- Do nice things for them at home like play games together or help
them with homework.
- Don't use your cancer to get attention or to avoid your chores.
Pitch in and help out as much as you can.
- Try to be nice to your brothers and sisters. It helps to remember
that you aren't the only one in the family having a hard time.

When you are feeling bad, it might be hard to understand why your
parents are paying so much attention to your brothers and sisters—
after all, they are feeling well! It helps to keep in mind that it is your
parents' job to care for all of the kids in the family.

**Here are some things you might
see your parents do to take care
of your brothers and sisters:**
- Explain to your brothers and sisters
about the cancer and the treatments.
Information helps; secrets hurt.
- Encourage you to share your gifts.
- Talk with all of the children about
how they are feeling.
- Don't let other people focus just
on you. Your brothers and sisters
need some attention, too.
- Give lots of hugs and kisses.
- Do fun things with your brothers and
sisters. One family had "out with the
parents" nights when each child would go
out with one parent all by themselves. The

kids got to pick where to go and what to do. It turned out that where they went didn't seem as important as having some time alone with their parent.

Grandparents

Grandparents often have a tough time when a grandchild is diagnosed with cancer. They have double worries. They worry about their own child (your mom or dad) and their grandchild (you). They also sometimes think that it's really unfair that they are healthy and you are sick. It sort of turns what everyone expects upside down. Most of the time, old people get sick and kids are healthy. Not the other way around.

One thing that helps grandparents a lot is information. They might not know that there are really good treatments for most kinds of cancers that kids get. If they go with your parents to talk with the doctor or read some of the books about kid's cancers, they might feel better. They might remember a child they knew many years ago who got cancer when there weren't good treatments. They might be really sad thinking about that. Once they know that there are good treatments for you, they might feel more hopeful.

Here are a few things that sometimes make grandparents feel better:
- Getting good information from your parents, your doctor, or books.
- Helping out with your brothers and sisters (this might keep them too busy to worry).
- Calling them from the hospital. Just hearing your voice will make them happy.
- Telling them, or writing to them, "I love you." This always helps!

Good friends

Most kids have a very best friend or several good friends. These are the kids you play with, have sleepovers with, and share your thoughts with. Good friends are like comfy pajamas—they just fit. Your best friend is the person you might call first to tell about what is happening to you. He or she might react to hearing that you have cancer in all sorts of ways, like:

- "I thought only old people got cancer." (Not true. Over 12,000 kids in the U.S. get cancer every year.)
- "Does that mean you are going to die?" (Nope, there are really good treatments these days.)
- "Can I catch cancer from you?" (Nope, can't happen. Even if your blood got into your best friend, cancer couldn't grow. You can't get it from sharing toothbrushes, a Popsicle, or anything else. Cancer isn't contagious.)
- "When will you feel better?" (Depends on the treatment you need. Ask your doctor how long it will be so you can tell everyone.)
- "Will your hair fall out?" (Depends on treatment. But if you need chemo or radiation to your head, your hair probably will fall out. But then it will grow back.)

Your friends will probably have lots more questions. You could read this book together, and write any questions you have in the end of the chapters. Then, you can get straight answers from your doctor or nurse.

Good friends can really brighten up your days. If you try to stay in touch by phone or email or visits, your best friend will share what you are going through. Your friend can tell you what's going on at school and in the neighborhood. Your friends also can help make sure other kids know the right information. Sometimes rumors start at schools and facts can get all mixed up. Your friend can say, "Nope, that's not right. Maria is at the hospital this week and she'll be home next week. I saw her and she's doing fine."

School friends

Getting back to school after your cancer treatment starts can be a real relief. It means something in your life is back to normal. You are back in the same classes, with the same teachers, and the same classmates. Some of the kids in your school are friends, others are acquaintances (you know their faces or names, but you don't play together much), and some are strangers. Of course, if you go to a very small school, you probably know everyone.

School may seem a little different when you go back, though. Acquaintances and strangers might be surprised to see you come back looking different than before. They might not know you have cancer and they might tease you. Or, if they do know you have cancer, they might not have the right facts. They might think they can catch it from you. Your close friends also might not act like themselves.

So, what can you do to get back to normal at school? The first thing to do is try to keep in touch when you are in the hospital.

Here are some things your parents can do to help with that:
- Tell your teacher and principal that you have cancer and are in the hospital.
- Call or email often to let them know how you are.
- Encourage your teacher to have your classmates send notes, email, or call on the phone.
- If you are going to be out of school for more than two weeks, make arrangements for a visiting teacher to come tutor you in the hospital or at home.

- Encourage your closest friends to come visit when you feel like having visitors.
- Make arrangements for the hospital nurse or school liaison to go with your parents to the school to explain about cancer to your classmates. Make sure all of your classmates' questions are answered.

There are lots of things you can do to let your friends at school know that you are the same old you. If you want, you can call or email them as soon as you can to tell them what's going on. You can explain that you have to take medicine or have surgery or get radiation. Make sure they know that cancer is not contagious—they can't catch it. If you feel like it, you can ask them if they want to visit. When they do, take them on a tour. Or even better, see if the child life specialist will go on the tour with you. Your friends will like meeting such a fun person. Maybe you can do some projects together in the recreation therapy room, eat in the cafeteria, or watch a movie together. Your friend might like to ride up and down in the hospital bed.

Here are a few more ideas:

- Call or email your classroom with "hospital updates."
- Send pictures or a scrapbook about the hospital to your class.
- Do a project for school called "What I learned in the hospital."
- Make a video to send to your classroom.

- Thank your teacher for whatever she does to help you keep in touch.

When you go back to school, wear a hat or scarf if you want. Explain what's been going on and make it sound interesting. Then try to get back to the normal stuff you used to do: work at your desk, play on the playground, and do your best.

Hospital friends

Have you ever thought about what makes a good friend? Usually, you make friends if you like the same things. You might love horses, and make friends with someone at the stable. Or, you might play basketball and make a best friend on the team. Sometimes you make friends because you gradually get to know someone who sits next to you in class. It might not be someone you ever dreamed you'd be friends with. But, over time, you learn that you laugh at the same things or like to read the same books.

You'll probably find that you make lots of friends at the hospital or clinic. First of all, you spend a lot of time there. So, you have a chance to get to know other kids in the hospital or in the clinic waiting room. Also, you are sharing the same experience. They know about throwing up from chemo more than the kids in school do. And, they are probably bald so they know what that feels like. They might even have tips on what to say to rude people ("Oh, this hairstyle is a special from Mr. Chemo") or what to do when you feel sick to your stomach (eat crackers and listen to music). They understand. Your hospital friends' parents might even make friends with your parents.

Friendships with other kids with cancer can be wonderful and painful. The wonderful part is that you meet lots of nice kids in hospitals. You learn all sorts of ways to deal with cancer from them. You can have lots of fun at popcorn parties in your room or sneak attacks on the resident doctors with silly string. Even on days when you feel lousy, they can probably make you laugh. Or if not, they can sit with you and talk. Or read you a book. Or just hold your hand.

One hard thing that can happen is if your friend gets sicker. Because you know what it feels like to be sick, it may be especially hard for you to watch your friend be sick. It might make you worry that you might get sicker, too. You can talk to your parents, counselor, favorite relative, or friend about how you are feeling.

You can write a letter to your friend about how special he or she is. Or you can list the funniest things he ever said to you. You can visit a lot and talk. You both might laugh thinking back on the silly string ambush or the no-hair Barbie parties. Or maybe just watch a movie together. You can talk to your counselor, or draw pictures about how you feel, or write in a journal.

Your hospital friends probably will get better, though. Most kids with cancer do these days. When you are finished with treatment, you and your hospital friends might drift apart or stay lifelong friends. Just as you might with the child who sits next to you in school.

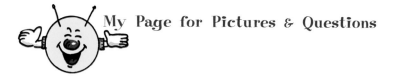 My Page for Pictures & Questions

Chapter 8

Life After Cancer

You are probably reading this book at the beginning of your cancer journey. It might be hard to imagine that treatment will end. But, after months or years of ups and downs, it will. And it can feel both exciting and strange.

This chapter talks a bit about the rest of your life after cancer, starting with your last day of treatment.

Last day

The exciting day has arrived: Your last trip to the clinic or hospital for treatment. It may feel both thrilling and scary that after all of the months or years of exams, procedures, and treatments, a new phase is beginning.

You can ask you doctor ahead of time what to expect on the last day of treatment. But usually the following things happen.

- The doctors and nurses give the last treatment.
- They congratulate you on doing such a great job during treatment. They might give you a certificate.
- They will go over the follow-up schedule with you and your parents.
- They will talk about when to have your central line removed (if you have one) and what that will be like.
- You can take "good bye" pictures of the doctors and nurses (even though you'll still see them for follow-up visits).

Some families want to mark this special occasion by bringing in a cake or cookies to share with the staff. Others just want to get it over with and go home.

The doctors and nurses will probably be very excited. They work hard to help kids get better. Your parents are probably pretty excited too. But, in all the joy, a little worry sometimes creeps in. After all of the constant care, stopping can be a little scary. Parents and children usually worry that the disease will come back. Just like during treatment, you can talk to your parents, your psychologist, or your friends about how you feel. Remember, you can have more than one feeling at a time. Usually, every person in the family has mixed emotions.

Lots of families have celebrations after the last day of treatment. Here are some ideas:
- Throw all of your left over medicines in the garbage and chant "Good bye, good bye."
- Give any usable supplies (heparin, bandages) to kids you know who are still getting treatment.
- Have a big party to thank everyone who helped you.
- Go on a vacation with your family.

Other families don't like to make a big deal about ending treatment. They just want to slip back into normal life. Talk about it together to see what everyone wants to do.

Usually, ending treatment means the surgeries, medicines, and radiation are finished. But you'll still need frequent check-ups. The first year you may need to get an exam and blood tests every month or two, and sometimes a scan. What you need depends on what kind of cancer you had. As time goes on, the visits will be less frequent. After a couple of years, you may only need a check-up once a year. If your parents ask the doctor for a schedule of appointments, you'll know what to expect.

Central line removal

Sometime after treatment ends, you'll have an appointment to have your central line removed. Some children feel attached to their central line and don't really want to have it taken out. Others can't wait for it to be gone. It's okay to feel either way.

But the day will come when it's time for it to come out. If you have an external catheter, the doctor will give you medicine to relax and then gently pull it out. It only takes a couple of minutes. The doctor will put a small bandage on the place where it used to be, and that's it.

If you have an implanted catheter, you'll need a short surgery to remove it. Your parents will make an appointment, and you won't be able to eat or drink for several hours before the surgery. Then you will get anesthesia through your central line or a mask. Be sure to ask the anesthesiologist if you'll get flavored gas with the mask. You might be able to pick your favorite flavor like bubble gum or grape.

I am so outta here!

While you are asleep, the surgeon will make a small incision, take out the catheter, then put a few stitches in. The surgeon will cover the stitches with a small bandage and they will take you to the recovery room to wake up. When you are wide-awake, the nurses might give you a drink or a Popsicle. Then you can go home.

Some children want to take the catheter home with them. Tell the surgeon if you'd like to do that. Some children put it in a drawer; others do things like make bracelets or Christmas ornaments out of it. Six-year-old Katy brought it home and pounded it with a hammer. Jose wanted the surgeon to throw it away. Whatever you want to do with the central line is okay.

Follow-up care

You'll probably see your regular oncologist and nurse practitioner for your after-treatment check-ups for two years, then you'll graduate to a follow-up program. These programs are usually at your same hospital but there may be different doctors and nurses who specialize in taking care of survivors. Their job is to help you stay healthy.

Your visit to the follow-up clinic will be like other visits to the doctor. You'll talk to the doctor and nurse and get a physical exam. You can tell them about the things in your life that are going well. You also can tell them about anything that is not going well or that you are worried about.

They will give you or your parent a summary of your treatment. It will include a list of the medicines you took and the total dosages, how much radiation you got and where, and the surgeries you had. It should include your follow-up schedule. It's important to keep your summary in a safe place since you will give a copy to each of your doctors for the rest of your life.

The doctors and nurses at follow-up clinics are experts in caring for survivors of childhood cancer. They help you stay well. Let's say you had a treatment that can affect your growth. They will keep a close watch on that by measuring how tall you are sitting down and standing up. They may do some special blood tests. If necessary, they will send you to a specialist (pediatric endocrinologist) who works with children to help them grow. Or, treatment might make you learn in a different way than you did before. In that case, the doctors will figure out the best way you learn and work with your school to help you to learn more easily.

For the rest of your life, you can call the follow-up clinic to find out anything you need to about your cancer treatment. Even when you are a grown up, you or your doctor can talk to these experts about what you can do to stay healthy.

The rest of your life

This book was a little guide through a tough time in your life: having cancer. When the cancer is gone, you will move on. You'll become a teenager, then an adult. Your cancer history may cause you to wonder about a lot of things as you mature:

Why did I get cancer?
Did it happen for a reason?
Did it make me a better person?
Am I a hero?
Am I a victim?
Am I a survivor or just a person who had cancer?

Different people have different answers for each of these questions. The beginning of this book talked about how unique you are. No one is exactly like you. And each person has different feelings and thoughts about having had cancer when they were young.

Your cancer doesn't change who you are inside. It doesn't make you a hero or a victim—just a human being who faced a big challenge. You had a huge experience at a young age. Just like kids who were in a big car accident or who were hurt in a flood, all children have events in their lives that affect who they become as adults. Having had cancer is one of these big events. It can play a part in how you view the world. However, it is just one of many things that shape who you are. There are almost a quarter of a million (yep, 250,000) people in the United States who share a history of childhood cancer.

You probably learned a lot going through cancer and treatments. You learned how quickly life can change and how many people care about you. You also learned skills that will help you in the future. You know that things can be managed, one day at a time. You know that you can ask questions so you are prepared to face anything that comes up. You know that you are tougher than you thought. And you know that sometimes everyone needs help.

After treatment ends you may think the worst is now behind you or you may worry about the future. As you've learned in this book, different people have very different feelings about different things and these feelings often change over time. But, the rest of your life is ahead of you and you have the opportunity to make the most of it.

As with most big experiences, there are things about having cancer that were hard and things that were good. When treatment is over, lots of kids look back and realize that the cancer changed their lives in positive ways. Some kids grow up to become doctors, nurses, or psychologists. Many stop worrying about little things and appreciate all of the goodness in their lives. Having been really sick can make you more aware of happy times. You might tell more jokes or laugh more. You will probably be kinder to kids in school who are a little bit different. Sometimes out of hard times, good things come.

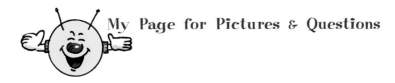 My Page for Pictures & Questions

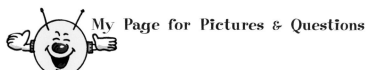My Page for Pictures & Questions

My Hospital Journal

My name_____

Date I came to the hospital_____

Name of hospital_____

Before I came to the hospital

What I thought it would be like_____

_____

_____

What my parents told me_____

_____

_____

The hospital tour_____

_____

_____

What I packed_____

_____

_____

_____

_____

My room

My room number_____

My bed_____

What I see out my window_____

_____

_____

_____

_____

How I decorated my room_____

_____

_____

_____

Why I am in the hospital

How my parents describe it_____

_____

_____

_____

_____

How my doctor describes it_____

_____

_____

_____

What I think of it_____

_____

_____

_____

_____

My doctor(s)

My doctor's name

What I call him/her

What I like best about my doctor

What I don't like

My doctor writes a note_____

_____

_____

_____

_____

My nurse(s)

My nurses' names_____

_____

What I call them_____

_____

What I like best about my nurses_____

_____

_____

_____

What I don't like _____

_____

_____

_____

My nurse writes a note _____

_____

_____

_____

_____

My roommate(s)

My roommate's name _____

_____

Why my roommate is in the hospital _____

_____

_____

Where my roommate lives _____

_____

_____

_____

What I like about sharing a room _____

_____

_____

_____

_____

_____

What I don't like _____

_____

_____

_____

_____

_____

My school

My teacher's name

My best friends at school

My favorite subject

How my class will know I'm in the hospital

How I do my homework

People who sent me cards or gifts

Friends sign in sheet

Relatives sign in sheet

Meals in the hospital

What I order for meals

Favorite breakfast

Favorite lunch

Favorite dinner

Food I don't like

How eating in the hospital is different form eating at home_____

_____

Foods I can't have_____

_____

_____

Places I've been to in the hospital

_____ Lobby

_____ Gift shop

_____ Cafeteria

_____ Playroom

_____ Clinic

_____ Elevator

_____ Operating room

_____ Recovery room

_____ Nurses' station

_____ X-ray room

Other places_____

_____

_____

_____

_____

_____

_____

_____

_____

_____

_____

What happens at night in the hospital

What it sounds like_____

_____

_____

_____

When the nurses come in_____

_____

_____

_____

What nurses do at night_____

_____

_____

_____

What I like_____

_____

_____

_____

_____

What I don't like_____

_____

_____

_____

What I miss from home

Brothers_____

_____

_____

Sisters_____

_____

_____

My pets_____

_____

_____

My friends_____

_____

_____

My bed_____

_____

What else?_____

_____

_____

Playing in the hospital

How I play in my room_____

_____

_____

_____

What the hospital playroom is like_____

_____

_____

_____

How I go to the playroom_____

_____

_____

_____

Who helps kids in the playroom

What toys are there

Other kids I met there

Medicine

Pills I have to take_____

_____

How the pills taste_____

_____

Liquid medicine I take_____

_____

How it tastes_____

_____

Shots of medicine_____

_____

How it feels_____

_____

_____

Medicines I take at home_____

_____

How I feel about my medicines_____

_____

Tests in the hospital

_____   CAT scan

_____   X-ray

_____   Blood draw

Others_____

_____

_____

Test I like the best_____

_____

_____

_____

Tests I don't like_____

_____

_____

Prizes I got_____

_____

_____

_____

_____

_____

_____

Operation

What my operation is for_____

_____

Where my scar is_____

_____

What my bandages look like_____

_____

How long my operation took_____

_____

My surgeon's name_____

_____

What I remember_____

_____

_____

_____

_____

_____

_____

_____

_____

Memories

What I remember most_____

How I'll feel when I come back to the hospital

Hospital Packing List

Your hospital may have given your parents a list of what they want you to bring to the hospital. For a short stay you won't need to pack much, but for a long boring stay you'll need to pack a lot of stuff to make it interesting. You can check the list below to see what you want to take.

Your parents can check with the hospital about whether there is anything on the list that you can't have in the hospital. For instance, your wonderfully germy bear or doll or soldier may need serious de-germing before you to take it to the hospital or the hospital may offer to de-germ it when you get there.

Clothing

_____ shirts

_____ pants

_____ underwear

_____ pajamas

_____ bathrobe

_____ slippers

_____ shoes

_____ socks

_____ hats

For the room

_____ blankets

_____ bedspread or quilt

_____ comfy pillow

_____ pictures of family, friends, pets

_____ favorite stuffed animal

_____ posters

_____ tape to put up pictures and posters

_____ latex-free balloons

_____ streamers, crepe paper

_____ books for parents and kids

_____ magazines

_____ scented creams and soaps

_____ stationary and stamps

_____ address book

_____ snack foods and drinks

_____ table lamp or nightlight

_____ flashlight

Toys

_____ dolls

_____ children's books

_____ playing cards

_____ dominoes

_____ puzzles

_____ water pistol

_____ light saber

_____ silly string

_____ puppets

_____ craft projects

_____ legos

_____ art kit (play doh, stickers, markers, cookie cutters, scissors, glue, clay, etc)

_____ video tapes

_____ tape player or CD boom box

_____ hand held computer games (game boy)

_____ extra batteries or charger

_____ audio tapes or CDs

_____ books on tape

_____ board games

_____ magic tricks (fake thumb!)

_____ glow in the dark

beach ball

_____ joke book

_____ pens, pencils, paper

Toiletries

_____ eye glasses

_____ toothbrush

_____ toothpaste

_____ dental floss

_____ tissues

_____ body lotion

_____ powder

_____ shampoo/

conditioner

_____ soap

_____ brush and comb

_____ nail clippers

_____ earplugs

Miscellaneous

_____ food

_____ camera and film

_____ money

_____ phone cards

_____ laptop computer

_____ sewing kit

(pocket size)

_____ safety pins

_____ hot water bottle

My Page for Pictures & Questions

Resources

Many resources exist for families of children with cancer. This appendix contains a sampling of some especially helpful organizations, books, videotapes, and online websites. To find a comprehensive list of resources, refer to the appendices of the books *Childhood Leukemia, Childhood Cancer,* or *Childhood Brain & Spinal Cord Tumors* listed below. You can find them in your local public library, at your local bookstore (if not on the shelf, they can order one for you), or from an online bookseller like www.amazon.com or www.bn.com.

ORGANIZATIONS

BMT Infonet
2900 Skokie Valley Road, Suite B
Highland Park, IL 60035
(888) 597-7674
http://www.bmtinfonet.org
Provides quality information and emotional support for people who need a bone marrow or stem cell transplant. They publish books, an excellent newsletter, and a drug database. They provide the best list of transplant resources on the Internet.

Candlelighters Childhood Cancer Foundation
PO Box 498
Kensington, MD 20895-0498
(800) 366-CCCF
http://www.candlelighters.org
Founded in 1970, Candlelighters has more than 100,000 members in the U.S. Some of the free services provided by Candlelighters are a toll-free information hotline, a quarterly newsletter, various handbooks to help families of children with cancer, local support group chapters, and national advocacy.

Leukemia & Lymphoma Society
1311 Mamaroneck Avenue
White Plains, NY 10605
(914) 949-5213 or (800)-955-4LSA
http://www.leukemia-lymphoma.org
This organization provides financial assistance to families (up to $500/year for out-patients), funds research, sponsors a national program in education for the public and the medical community, and publishes a large number of booklets on cancer-related topics.

National Cancer Institute (NCI)
Bethesda, MD 20892
(800) 4-CANCER
http://www.cancer.gov
http://www.cancer.gov/cancer_information/pdq
Provides a nationwide telephone service for people with cancer, their families and friends, and the professionals who treat them. The NCI answers questions and sends out informational booklets on a variety of cancer-related topics. PDQ is the National Cancer Institute's computerized listing of accurate and up-to-date information for patients and health professionals about cancer treatments, research studies and clinical trials.

For a list of brain tumor organizations, visit the webpage of the North American Brain Tumor coalition at http://www.nabraintumor.org.

BOOKS FOR CHILDREN

Baker, Lynn, MD. *You and Leukemia: A Day at a Time.* Philadelphia: W.B. Saunders Company, 2nd ed. 2002. Warm book about many aspects of childhood leukemia. Chapter 4 contains clear descriptions of procedures and treatments for both children and adults.

Foss, Karen. *The Problem with Hair: A Story for Children Learning about Cancer.* Centering Corporation, 1996. A poem/story about a group of friends and what happens when one of them loses her hair from chemotherapy.

Krisher, Trudy. *Kathy's Hats: A Story of Hope.* Concept Books, 1992. (800-255-7675). A charming book for ages 5 to 10 about a girl whose love of hats comes in handy when chemo makes her hair fall out.

Rey, Margaret and H.A. Rey. *Curious George Goes to the Hospital.* New York: Houghton Mifflin, 1966. Curious George needs to go to the hospital for an operation.

Richmond, Christina. *Chemo Girl: Saving the World One Treatment at a Time.* Jones and Bartlett Publishers, 1996. Written by a 12-year-old with rhabdomyosarcoma, this book describes a superhero who shares hope and encouragement.

Rogers, Fred. *Going to the Hospital.* New York: G. P. Putnam's Sons, 1997. With pictures and words, TV's beloved Mr. Rogers helps children ages 3 to 8 learn about hospitals.

Rogers, Fred. *Some Things Change and Some Things Stay the Same.* American Cancer Society (800) ACS-2345. Very comforting book for children with cancer and their siblings.

Romain, Trevor. *Bullies are a Pain in the Brain.* Minneapolis, MN: Free Spirit Publishing, 1997. Full of warmth and whimsy, this book teaches children skills to cope with teasing and bullying.

Saltzman, David. *The Jester has Lost his Jingle.* Jester Co, Inc., 1995. The jester sets out to find the laughter missing in his kingdom. On his journey, he teaches young children about how positive thinking can help overcome difficulties.

Shultz, Charles. *Why, Charlie Brown, Why?* New York: Topper Books, 1990. Tender story of a classmate who develops leukemia. Available as a book or videotape. Leukemia & Lymphoma Society, (800) 955-4LSA.

BOOKS FOR ADULTS

Keene, Nancy. *Childhood Leukemia: A Guide for Families, Friends, and Caregivers.* 3rd edition. O'Reilly & Associates, 2002. Provides comprehensive, accurate, and up-to-date information for families of children with leukemia. Includes the stories of over 100 parents, children with leukemia, and their siblings.

Janes-Hodder, Honna & Nancy Keene. *Childhood Cancer: A Parent's Guide to Solid Tumor Cancers.* 2nd edition. O'Reilly & Associates, 2002. Provides comprehensive, accurate, and up-to-date information for families of children with solid tumors (except brain and spinal cord tumors). Includes the stories of over 100 parents, children with solid tumors and their siblings.

Shiminski-Mahar, Cullen, Sansalone. *Childhood Brain & Spinal Cord Tumors: A Guide for Families, Friends, and Caregivers.* O'Reilly & Associates, 2002. Provides comprehensive, accurate, and up-to-date information for families of children with brain and spinal cord tumors. Includes the stories of over 100 parents, children with brain tumors, and their siblings.

Keene, Hobbie, Ruccione. *Childhood Cancer Survivors: A Practical Guide to Your Future.* O'Reilly & Associates, 2000. A user friendly, comprehensive guide on late effects of treatment for childhood cancer. Full of stories from survivors of all types of childhood cancer. Also covers emotional issues, insurance, jobs, relationships, and ways to stay healthy.

Stewart, Susan. *Bone Marrow Transplants: A Book of Basics for Patients.* Published by BMT InfoNet (888) 597-7674, (847) 433-3313, or http://www.bmt-news.org. 157-page book clearly explains all medical aspects of bone marrow transplantation, the different types of transplants, emotional and psychological considerations, pediatric transplants, complications, and insurance issues. Technically accurate, yet easy to read.

Stewart, Susan. *Autologous Stem Cell Transplants: A Handbook for Patients.* BMT InfoNet, 2000. Order by calling (888) 597-7674, (847) 433-3313, or visiting http://www.bmtnews.org.

VIDEOS FOR CHILDREN

Why, Charlie Brown, Why? Tender story of a classmate who develops leukemia. Available as a book or videotape. For video availability, call the Leukemia and Lymphoma Society, (800) 955-4LSA.

Hairballs on my Pillow. CARTI. P.O. Box 55050, Little Rock, AR 72215. (800) 482-8561 or (501) 664-8573. Videotape shows interviews of children with cancer and their friends discussing friendship and returning to school. $35 for video and newsletters for students, exercises and activities for students, and a teachers notebook of information about cancer and its treatment, dealing with returning students, and additional resources.

Mr. Rogers Talks About Childhood Cancer. 1990. Videotapes (2), guidebook, storybook. 45 mins. VHS. Available from American Cancer Society. (800) ACS-2345. Mr. Rogers talks to children and uses characters from the land of make believe to stress the importance of talking about feelings.

VIDEOS FOR OLDER CHILDREN AND TEENS

What Am I-Chopped Liver? Video with attitude from the Starbright Foundation. Helps teens deal with their doctor in a proactive and age-appropriate manner. (310) 442-1560 ext. 10 or http://www.starbright.org.

Plastic Eggs or Something!?. Video with attitude from the Starbright Foundation. It offers insight into and strategies for dealing with hospital life, such as making friends with the hospital staff, dealing with the many boring hours, and finding a little privacy in the hospital. Free to teens with cancer. 310-442-1560 ext. 10 or http://www.starbright.org.

Rising to the Challenge: Youngsters Speak Their Truth with Cancer. 15 minute video that depicts the thoughts and feelings of children with cancer, ages 10 and older, filmed during a rafting trip. Aquarius Healthcare Videos (888) 420-2963, http:www.aquariusproductions.com.

VIDEOS FOR ADULTS

Cancervive Back to School Kit. A comprehensive package of materials developed to assist children and adolescents re-entering the school setting. The kit contains a "Teachers Guide for Kids with Cancer" and two award-winning documentary videos, "Emily's Story: Back to School After Cancer" and "Making the Grade: Back to School After Cancer for Teens." http://www.cancervive.org/materials.html Item No. 123 ($79.95).

Financial Management During Crisis. Healthcare providers, utility and credit companies, and families of seriously ill children tell how to sucessfully manage your insurance, work with creditors, establish a workable budget, and find outside help. 24 minutes. Aquarius Healthcare Videos (888) 420-2963, http://www.aquariusproductions.com. ($140).

The Trish Greene Back to School Program for Children with Cancer. Designed to increase communication among healthcare professionals, parents, patients and school officials to assure a smooth transition from active treatment back to school and daily life. Materials, videos and other printed inventory are available at all local chaptersof the Leukemia & Lymphoma Society. http://www.leukemia-lymphoma.org or (800) 955-4LSA. Free.

No Fears, No Tears. By Leora Kuttner, PhD. Documentary of eight young children with cancer and their parents about learning how to manage the pain of cancer treatment. 27 minutes. Distributed by Fanlight Distributors (800) 937-4113 or sandy@fanlight.com

Mr. Rogers Talks with Parents About Childhood Cancer. Videotapes (2), guidebook, pamphlet. The first tape consists of interviews with parents about ways to deal with emotions during diagnosis and treatment. The second tape includes sensitive interviews with three bereaved parents. 47 minutes. Available at some chapters of the American Cancer Society. (800) ACS-2345. Free.

FUN THINGS TO WEAR

Just in Time. Makes reversible all-cotton headwear for women and girls ages 7 to 12. To order call (215) 247-8777 or visit online at http://www.softhats.com.

Hip Hats. Provides hats with human hair that are soft, comfortable, and fun to wear. To order call (877) 447-4287 or (813)-229-2377 outside of U.S. for a free catalog.

ONLINE RESOURCES

ACOR, The Association of Cancer Online Resources, Inc.
http://www.acor.org
ACOR offers access to 131 mailing lists that provide support, information, and community to everyone affected by cancer and related disorders. It hosts several pediatric cancer discussion groups, including PED-ONC (a general pediatric cancer discussion group), ALL-KIDS (childhood acute lymphoblastic leukemia), and PED-ONC SURVIVORS (for parents of survivors).

Bandaids and Blackboards-When Chronic Illness Goes to School
http://www.faculty.fairfield.edu/fleitas/sitemap.html
Wonderful, fun, and informative website about ill children and school.

Pediatric Oncology Resource Center
http://www.acor.org/ped-onc
Edited by Patty Feist-Mack, this site is the best single source of information for families about pediatric cancers on the Internet. It contains detailed and accurate material on diseases, treatment, family issues, activism, and bereavement. It also provides links to helpful cancer sites.

Squirreltales
http://www.squirreltales.com/
An uplifting and practical website to encourage and empower parents of children with cancer when they are feeling discouraged and powerless.

Musella Foundation for Brain Tumor Research and Information
http://www.virtualtrials.org
This site contains an enormous amount of medical, practical, and resource information for people with brain tumors.

WISH TRIP ORGANIZATIONS

Make-a-Wish Foundation of America
3350 North Central Avenue, Suite 300
Phoenix, AZ 85012
(602) 279-WISH or (800) 722-WISH
http://www.wish.org
U.S. and international chapters and affiliates. Grants wishes to children under the age of eighteen with life-threatening illnesses.

The Starlight Children's Foundation
5900 Wilshire Boulevard, Suite 2530
Los Angeles, CA 90036
(323) 634-0080
http://www.starlight.org
Has chapters in the United States, Canada, Australia, and United Kingdom. Fulfills wishes for seriously ill children ages four to eighteen.

A comprehensive list of wish fulfillment organizations can be found on the Web at http://www.patientcenters.com/leukemia/.

CAMPS FOR KIDS WITH CANCER

Children's Oncology Camping Associates International
http://www.coca-intl.org/
An international organization of people providing camping experiences for children with cancer.

Pediatric Oncology Resource Center
http://www.acor.org/ped-onc/cfissues/camps.html
Maintains a list of camps for children with cancer organized by state and province.

BEREAVEMENT

Grollman, Earl. *Talking About Death: A Dialogue Between Parent and Child.* 3rd ed. Boston: Beacon Press, 1991. One of the best books for helping children cope with grief. It contains a children's read-along section to explain and explore children's feelings. In very comforting language, this book teaches parents how to explain death, understand children's emotions, understand how children react to specific types of death, and know when to seek professional help. It also contains a resource section.

Schaefer, Dan, and Christine Lyons. *How Do We Tell the Children?: A Step-by-Step Guide for Helping Children Two to Teen Cope When Someone Dies.* New York: Newmarket Press, 3rd ed. 2002. If your terminally ill child has siblings, read this book. In straightforward, uncomplicated language, the authors describe how to explain the facts of death to children and teens and show how to include the children in the family support network, laying the foundation for the healing process to begin. Also includes a crisis section, for quick reference on what to do in a variety of situations.

Romain, Trevor. *What on Earth Do You Do When Someone Dies?* Minneapolis MN: Free Spirit Publishing, 1999. Warm, honest words and beautiful illustrations help children understand and cope with grief.

Talking about Death with Children. 13 minute videotape. Dr. Earl Grollman explains what death means, how it happens, and why there is a funeral. Includes a tour of a funeral home. Batesville Management Services. (800) 446-2504 ext 7788 ($99).

About Candlelighters

Candlelighters Childhood Cancer Foundation was formed in 1970. Parents of children who were being treated for cancer met in the basement of Children's Hospital (in Washington D.C.), where they talked with each other about their child's treatments. They realized when they shared ideas with other parents, that they felt better and were able to help their children more. Local chapters were then formed to provide support programs in each state across the country.

The name of the organization came from an old Chinese proverb, "It is better to light a candle than to curse the darkness." It expressed the goal of the organization: to identify the problems associated with childhood cancer and to take steps towards making them better. The National Office informs members of congress about the special needs of childhood cancer patients and publishes books and newsletters to teach families about childhood cancer. They have a toll-free hot line to answer questions and provide helpful information. Today, Candlelighters National Office and 275 local chapters across the country continue to support thousands of childhood cancer families each year. This book is written to help children between the ages of 6 and 12.

Candlelighters believes that children cope better and feel better when they understand their disease and the treatments. This book was commissioned to fill a large gap in educational materials. It contains practical and medical information to help children make sense of what is happening to them.

About This Book

The words of *Chemo, Crazies, and Comfort* were written by Nancy Keene and the illustrations were done by Trevor Romain. Dick Reeves of Dick Reeves Design (dreeves3@austin.rr.com) designed the interior layout and the cover. Fonts in the interior design are Goudy, Piffeo and Comic Sans. The layout was prepared using QuarkXpress and Photoshop on a MacIntosh G3 computer.

The book was edited by Mary Ellen Keene and copyedited by Doris Keene and Ruth Hoffman. Ruth Hoffman conducted quality assurance checks.